WHAT IS REAL
The Life and Crimes
of Darnell Riley

RILEY PEREZ

WHAT IS REAL
The Life and Crimes
of Darnell Riley

A Barnacle Book | Rare Bird Books
Los Angeles, Calif.

A Genuine Barnacle Book

A Barnacle Book | Rare Bird Books
453 South Spring Street, Suite 302
Los Angeles, CA 90013
rarebirdbooks.com

FIRST TRADE PAPERBACK ORIGINAL EDITION

Set in Minion
Printed in the United States

10 9 8 7 6 5 4 3 2 1

Publisher's Cataloging-in-Publication data
Names: Perez, Riley, author.
Title: What is Real? the Life and Crimes of Darnell Riley / Riley Perez.
Description: First Trade Paperback Original Edition | A Barnacle Book |
New York, NY; Los Angeles, CA: Rare Bird Books, 2018.
Identifiers: ISBN 9781947856264
Subjects: LCSH Perez, Riley. | Riley, Darnell. | Prisoners—United States—
California—Biography. | Prisons—United States—California—Anecdotes. |
Corrections—California—Anecdotes. | Extortion. | BISAC BIOGRAPHY &
AUTOBIOGRAPHY / Criminals & Outlaws.
Classification: LCC HV9468.P47 2018 | DDC 365/.44/092

"What is REAL?" asked the Rabbit one day....
Said the Skin Horse, "...Generally, by the time you are real,
most of your hair has been loved off, and your eyes drop out,
and you get all loose in the joints and very shabby. But these
things don't matter at all, because once you are real you can't
be ugly, except to people who don't understand."

The Velveteen Rabbit by Margery Williams is a story I've read
many times. I have had ten years to myself to read it again.
I realize now that it's not always what you look at, it's what you see.

Contents

Prologue

I WAS ACCUSTOMED TO waking five minutes before the three calls of pan-pan heralds in the new day. Being an early riser had become a badge of honor, which allowed me to flirt with the notion that my early rise provided me an advantage in whatever task that landed on my calendar.

Being an early riser allowed me time to study L as she slept. She was always naked, and where I enjoyed the comfort of layers of blankets, L only required a pillow positioned between her legs. Even on the nights when she would engage in battle with imaginary enemies, the pillow remained in place. I would wake her by tugging at the pillow, to see if it was cemented to her knees, but on this day, I didn't.

L was an easy read. Her permagrin, I knew it was the result of an affair she was contemplating. Once, I flippantly remarked that the smile was the result of a fantasy where she was being pleased by a Spanish Fighting Bull—L did not take kindly to my joke.

Thankfully the showerhead was positioned at a conventional height so that the water could be distributed across my body without me having to stoop down. I recited my customary prayer in thanks of the maintenance man charged with the water heater's upkeep.

The day progressed the same as every other. I chose not to wake L as I left; the smile remained fixed to her face and the pillow continued to provide proper hip balance. L was safe and secure as she wandered in thought.

Driving Franklin Avenue is usually a sign of being a voyeur or an exhibitionist, but at 5:30 a.m. I'm spared the fishbowl feeling that accompanies Hollywood traffic. On my drive west, I considered the mantra that I had adopted: 2005 is my year and nothing else exists. Prior to the calendar turning its back on 2004, every day of my life had been filled with the planning, the execution, or the covering up of one crime or another—2005 was the year I would walk away from all that.

I wasn't beholden to anyone and I knew that I wouldn't be lured back into any schemes by an old associate. Anyone who believed that they owed me a debt, I considered the debt forgiven. It was the only way to disconnect: I had to forgive all debts, or I would never be free of crime.

I was a year removed from my last criminal act and as far as I knew it was a cold case. I committed the crime in the exclusive community of Bel Air, California. No doors or windows were busted, no alarms were set off during entrance or exit. The marked man returned as expected and was quickly subdued. He never saw my face, never heard my voice. I wore gloves, and no prints were left. There was nothing to lead the authorities to me.

Frankie and I had been consulting for a wealthy housewife locked in a protracted war more officially referred to as a divorce. All we had to do was get the soon-to-be ex to understand that the amount the housewife was entitled to and the amount that she was requesting really weren't that far apart, and if an agreement could be made without both sides losing out in attorney's fees—well, wouldn't that be a whole lot easier? The housewife lived in Bel Air, just blocks away from the scene of my last crime. I drove by the home daily. In fact, I knew the victim; he patronized my gambling business, and I had been an invited guest at his home on occasion. My familiarity with him was the reason that I was chosen to carry out the crime.

After hours of debate, I left Bel Air, and as I drove past the well-manicured lawns and stately homes—a particular one was familiar—I thought of how fooled the entire community had been by the illusion of security. Even with cameras, iron gates, and armed men, there always existed the chance for technological or human error. Couple those possibilities with an ambitious and creative mind, and the security practically vanishes before your eyes. But those concerns were now behind me.

I'd thought about being free from criminal association a lot lately. At a red light or in an elevator, whenever there was a moment to myself, I thought of how foreign my former life had become. I had finally aligned my actions with the image that everyone had of me: a citizen. A John Doe. A Mr. So-and-So from up the street.

I pulled into the driveway, hoping to surprise L. Unlike in the past, I didn't retrieve my pistol from my glove compartment—the thought didn't cross my mind. Before I was up the porch stairs, I noticed a van racing up the cobblestone driveway, stopping less than ten feet from me. Two middle-aged men exited the van barking orders, though I couldn't hear the words their mouths formed— it was as if they were mutes. An army of bodies appeared in my peripheral view and before I could turn and focus, the two men in front of me had their handguns trained on me.

The sound began to come back: "Do not move. We are US Marshalls!"

The feel of the metal tightening on my wrist intensified as I focused on the clanking of the five ridges needed to properly secure me. The sound overpowered the questions being posed to me as I slowly laid face down on the ground. Two of the men consulted some paperwork. The smaller of the two men stepped forward, pushing the other men to the side.

"You're Darnell Riley." He nodded his head yes, wanting me to agree with his statement. I didn't answer, so he turned the page so that my image was staring back at me.

While sitting in the back of the van, I asked the older man that sat behind the wheel, "What is this for?"

"You're just another body, the first one this week," he replied without much concern for how I would receive the news. "We are just body baggers."

My grandfather had officially adopted me and my name is Darnell Riley Perez, but he and everyone in my life referred to me as Riley. The name Darnell was rarely uttered.

Riley Perez had no criminal interaction. Riley Perez was without sin. And that is how most people knew me.

As we backed out of the driveway, the officer asked me once again, "Are you Darnell Riley?"

Whatever name they wanted to call me wasn't going to delay me getting to the next stage of this journey. I responded, "Yes."

Confinement

"Once upon a midnight dreary."—Edgar Allen Poe

I SAT ALONE, CONFINED to a disagreeably damp holding cell. The officers traversed the hall, their boots and keys clanking with musical synchronicity. I thought that I would finally have a moment to question my thoughts, but the slamming of cell doors and the constant echoing of names being summoned never let up. There was a pattern building with the accused, as they got rushed from their holding cells into wood-paneled courtrooms, then off to staging areas, back down dirt-stained hallways—then quiet.

Loneliness is a shifting concept. I was alone in my journey but never actually left to myself for more than five minutes. My new companion, an ash-ridden man, entered the holding cell, carried by knobby knees that nearly buckled beneath his skeleton frame as he made his way to an open bench. He drifted into a coma-like trance and the snoring began, accompanied by violent bursts of gassy air. The ashy man slept and shook, as I looked on.

Ten minutes elapsed before the ashy man found the strength to stand. He stood on shaky legs and for the first time acknowledged that I was sharing the space with him. Not forgetting his character as the feeble jail addict, he resumed his shaking. I offered him the apple I had left from the cruel excuse of a meal they'd left earlier and the addict stopped shaking long enough to say, "No thanks, I'm kicking heroin." I looked on as the shaking resumed. The dingy blue LA County Jail jumpsuit engulfed his body like he were in his eternal coffin. "I'm tired of this shit…this life…" And so began his confession. I nodded every twenty words to act interested, my fear being that if he started slicing at his arms with a razor, there would be no way for me to explain this to the authorities. He carried on with his story and I was relieved that he didn't have the courage to end his life.

He would make his confessions, stretching back over forty years of "slamming junk…" He talked and I nodded every twenty words to act interested.

I was saved by a visit from my attorney. I took the interruption as a gift and excused myself from the heroin tales. Ron Richards was a brilliant attorney. He had little room for dancing around the severity of what I was facing, so in order of charges in the indictment, he rambled on at warp speed. I heard little of what he said until "…you are facing two life sentences without the possibility of parole." I was aware of the charges, but hearing them repeated caused my legs to go numb. I pondered the heroin route the old man had told me about—maybe I could end it all—and then I remembered that I detest needles and I am a fuckup and would probably error the shot and be a vegetable forever.

Returning from the self-induced horror film that I was directing in my mind, I heard Ron repeat the severity of the charges. The words individually are benign, but once arraigned in the sentence, the events the words describe become ghoulish. A humming buzz seized my mind and the last parts of his monologue settled in, and before I could ask questions he was gone.

I remember little of what he said once the buzzing started. My ashy companion started a conversation to fill the dead air. In his deliberate, measured tone, the confessions poured out of how he began his affair with heroin. I don't remember asking, or if he sensed my eagerness to escape, but he went on with the tales of the seductive "dog food" as he called it at times. He recalled fond memories of using and being used by the "bitch." The caesuras in his speech were maddening, as if for the first time he were relieving himself of the burden of his experiences. All the overdoses he came close to not returning from, the missed opportunities.

I asked, "What was too much?"

He didn't answer. His head shook in disagreement with what he knew I was asking of him. The fright of being in a hell that I can't end with suicide seized my thoughts—how terribly depressing it would be if the system removed suicide as an option.

Before I could make any further inquiries, my junkie companion relieved himself of the built-up gas. No excuses were rendered, no attempts to conceal the foul act made. Realizing his role in life as the perpetual junkie, the shaking resumed and he retired to the bench, leaving me to consult his odors and myself.

The old man slept for what seemed to be an eternity. The loneliness became maddening. I'd been hoping to have some type of interaction with the old man. Before I could adjust to the new feeling of despair, in walked a young Hispanic inmate. He walked in a mummy, stutter step. He sat and said nothing. I said nothing in return. Minutes passed, then several officers came to retrieve the kid, shackling him at his legs and wrists and connecting the chains to his waist. No one spoke. The kid complied without incident, clearly practiced at this ritual. Then, in a whisper that was positively menacing, he said, "They're going to kill me…I have life." He repeated the word life. The vacant look remained in his stare. He was stuck on the word, not talking to anyone in particular, but saying it as if he had just heard it for the first time.

His escorts extracted him from the cell and he continued with his study of the word "life." With each step his youthful appearance became hardened. Whatever he meant by "They're going to kill me…" was the end of everything he's got and everything he'll never have. I possibly just witnessed a kid who may never have the luxury of being with a woman. Why was he about to die, and who was going to kill him?

Booking

BECOMING INMATE NUMBER 8511329 was a blur. Where were the eight million people who came before me? I was sure that I would see the fingerprints of the men that came before me as I began my journey with escorts from the cramped halls and cells. I didn't know if it was day or night. There were no windows in the county lockup, no clocks on the walls to compare with my body's natural rhythm. Every time I managed to drift off into sleep, something resembling my name would be called and I would be told to report to the next line that was forming to continue the booking process.

A skinny teen was ushered from one room by several officers clearly skilled in administering pain. An officer off to the side reminded the group that "Anyone who wants to test their nuts can step up and get fucked." I knew that I wanted to maintain the structural integrity of my scrotum, and I decided to comply with the orders at every stage.

We were asked to disrobe. Or, as the deputy said, "Take your fucking clothes off! Keep your fucking mouths shut!" We packed our clothes into plastic bags labeled with our names and booking numbers. Upward of fifty naked bodies were crammed into a holding cell that may have been intended to hold fewer than ten. Everyone tried to remain motionless as the body heat added to the already musty air. Time stood still in the tiny space, and as an added punishment, the door opened and the officers deposited more naked bodies.

This was my existence: standing in cramped spaces with naked, violent men. I was told to stand, and I did. Two square feet of space was all I had. The combination of the men and their odors had me questioning what was real and what I might be imagining. I was deep into an exercise of olfactory imagery, hoping to get past the musty air: petrol fumes, fresh cut grass, a handful of coffee beans. The exercise wasn't working. Musty air overpowered my memory.

We were released from the cell after thirty minutes and allowed a bone-chilling two-minute shower. If it were a religious ceremony, the shower would've served as a baptism into the afterworld. The next five hours I lived what you imagine life to be in purgatory. I was neither dead nor alive, just existing in flux.

I jockeyed to claim a corner wall next to a vagabond who seemed all too eager to be in jail. I was prepared to withstand the odor that rose off my new companion's body, but my name was called and without delay, I followed the line that I was assigned to.

We ascended a flight of stairs, continued up a broken escalator, and were told to "Sit the fuck down!" The line stopped long enough for me to ponder why all of the officer's commands were delivered with the word "Fuck!"

Before I could develop any solid theory, my group was told to follow another group of inmates up a flight of stairs, and to stop at the red line and wait for the next orders. Guards were positioned at strategic locations throughout hallways, interrogating every inmate that passed that had visible tattoos. Gang affiliations were catalogued, housing assignments adjusted accordingly. Cell numbers were assigned to names and without much direction, inmates stepped out of line as if they were familiar with the routine. I was lost, so I followed the guy ahead of me, not knowing if he were leading me to my death.

I was told that I was in the old county jail, which I would come to see had multiple layers. The Old Glass house and the Twin Towers make up the downtown LA County Jail lockup. The sprawling Wayside facility in Saugus, California, next to the Six Flags theme park, served as the satellite facility, housing thousands of inmates. I had yet to see the theme park, so I had to be in one of the two downtown holes.

There are cells that house one, four, or six men, as well as living areas with limited dorm-style living in the downtown lockups. The single-man cells are reserved for suicide watch or an inmate housed on a high-security status. The cells all appear to be the same size, regardless of how many beds are docked in them. One could spread their arms the same in a one- or six-man cell and it would be possible to reach the wall. In the cells the toilet-sink unit sits positioned at the back of the cell for privacy. A phone is bolted to the wall next to the toilet and only makes collect calls. The bunks are stacked pancake style, leaving little room for movement. Step twice in any direction and you've got the entire cell covered.

Five men were already occupying my assigned cell when I arrived. Two older Hispanic gangster types sat on a lower bunk exchanging war stories. Two young Africans and an older African American man feigned focus on their card game. I walked in, not caring to greet my new mates. I sat my belongings on the empty bunk and without much care for what anyone else in the cell might want to share with me, I contorted my body into a knot and slipped into a deep sleep.

I was awakened by the older man. I did not know if it was morning or night, though the two Hispanic gangsters were out of the cell. The two younger guys that played cards with the older man were suspiciously positioned at the cell door, while the older man questioned me.

Fully aware of the serious nature of his questions, I focused on this man with the brutish mask in front of me. I would've viewed his massive head as comical if he weren't quite so close and instead I remained silent, waiting to see what would happen next. His bugged eyes conveyed the urgency of the talk that he wanted to have. The brute extended his hand, which I met with a fist bump—I didn't refuse his handshake or disregard his gesture altogether, but, my fist bump was a mask, as I knew a refusal to embrace would cause offense. I also knew from the last days of the booking process that I didn't want to shake hands with just anyone. I had witnessed men hide and retrieve items from cavities the Creator never intended to serve as storage units. The ease with which this all occurred made it clear that this was an accepted practice, one that I had no intention of participating in anytime soon. I knew the trick in the embrace with the brute would be to make the knuckles touch head-on and avoid the double-touch of the traditional pound-shake. I'd have to do it with ease to move the action along and get to the point.

The bugged-eyed brute seemed to be the spokesman for anyone with black skin in the cell that we occupied and embraced the position with much pride. I looked on as his lips moved, yet I couldn't make out exactly what he was saying. He adjusted his face and lowered his voice to a barely audible whisper. "Hey, who you run with?" Having been a juvenile delinquent familiar with the nerve testing that comes with confinement in youth penal institutions, I knew the wrong answer could land me in the infirmary. My rudimentary understanding of the rules allowed me to answer in the same low register, taking care in not allowing a hint of venom or contempt to surface.

The brute wasn't my ideal roommate, but I would come to see that he was doing his job. If I were aligned with his gang, then he would be responsible for my actions. The brute's attempt to understand who I was and who I chose to associate with was vital to maintain order in this world.

My answer stumbled out, "I'm an Other."

Without much thought to my answer, he continued, "My name is Brick. I'm from East Coast Crip. Check it out: we don't go to yard except on Mondays and Wednesdays—that's when all the brothas on this block all know to go out. The South Siders got to go every day, so they always have numbers on the yard."

The morning meal hadn't been served to our cells yet. Brick let me know our two Hispanic cellmates were at the yard (I would later find out that the yard was on the roof, caged in with a fenced gate canopy), so that would put the time between 4:00 a.m. and 5:00 a.m. Brick said "chow" would be given to us by 6:00 a.m. I would finally be able to adjust my thoughts and body rhythm.

Brick focused his attention to me and asked, "What are you Puerto Rican, Cuban or something?"

I replied, "Yeah." I worked to keep the conversation brief, so that I could fall back into a deep sleep. I never heard the names of the two youths that stood on guard. Brick continued with his rambling, going on with endless rules that governed life in the "county."

Brick was eager to reveal the knowledge he held regarding the inner Crip wars that stretch back to the early eighties and their long-standing enemy, the Bloods. Brick revealed in stages how the Mexican street gangs have been added to the civil war as a result of the various factions trying to control the drug trade.

The two factions within the Crip organization locked in a battle for supremacy are the Neighborhoods and the Gangsters. The Neighborhoods (NH/NHC) refer to themselves as Hoods, Hoostas, and Rolling, and the vernacular updates as phrases catch on with the group. The Neighborhoods' umbrella encompasses the Harlem 30s, Rolling 40s, 60s, 90s, the East Coast Crips, and the various cliques that line the stretch of the city where the East Coast have a presence.

The Gangsters (GC)—or as they prefer to be called, Gangstas— are a crew made up of any Crip gang that has gangsta in its name before the word Crip. The list is as wide as the Neighborhoods. The 42, Avalons, 43rd (Four Trey), 83rd (Eight Trey), the Main Street, Marvin Gardens, the Mansfield Gangstas, and the list goes on and on. An addition or deletion may play into a lesser-known Crip gang, but these gangs have operated in Los Angeles since the mid-seventies and have been the trendsetters that took LA gang culture to other states in the eighties.

Several other Crip gangs don't fall into the definitive NH or GC categories and may align with either group or stay neutral and focus on the Bloods. The Hoover Gang (Hoova) defies Crip tradition and remains a Gang unto themselves. They associate with GCs, and their gang stretches the length of Hoover Street from their oldest clique at 43rd street. They have the 52 (Five Deuce), 77th, 83rd, 92nd, and the 112th. The Hoova Gang has a long bloodied history versus the NH Crips. The Rolling 60s are their mortal enemy, which has made for an alliance with several Blood Gangs that have been locked in a protracted war with the 60s.

The neighborhoods where these gangs run their operation are streets away from some of the wealthiest areas in California. It is painfully obvious that any attempt to define LA by its neighborhood or district will fall short of fully painting the definitive story of LA. Brick took great joy in serving as the official historian for the shifting gang sectors of LA. The minutes moved on, and, surprisingly, Brick proved to be a proficient storyteller.

The curious side of my mind would've had me stay up and engage Brick in a marathon interview as I realized that his vault of information could serve as a National Geographic guide to the hood, allowing gangsters and civilians to stay up to date on the ever-changing alliances and back-alley deal making. For a gangbanger, knowing where your gang is housed in the LA County Jail is as important as knowing what neighborhoods to avoid. Agreeing to be housed on a floor that your enemy controls is a virtual death sentence.

Brick talked to another inmate down the cellblock named Rick Rock. Rick Rock screamed out to Brick, "What's up, Hood Star?" The term indicated this cellblock was maintained by the NHC. I would later find out that the NHC have control of the 2,000 and 3,000 floors. There are pockets of each floor that house GCs and Hoovas. It is common knowledge for the regular residents which gang rules which floor. A Blood can be on the 4,000 floor, but generally will avoid the NH-controlled 2,000 and 3,000 floors, as most every Blood gang has a rival NH Crip gang as an enemy.

The Southern Mexican Gangs (South Siders as they call themselves, or Sureños/SS) are housed all throughout the county jail and unify under the Sureño flag. Whatever their street gang affiliations, once incarcerated, they only represent Sureño. Several Southern gangs are at odds with the SS, so they are housed in separate cellblocks. The Mara Villa Gang, which is one of the oldest Mexican gangs in LA, refuses to follow the draconian rules that the Mexican Mafia imposes on all SS. For their refusal to align with all the rules, they have been placed on the "Greenlight"—otherwise known as marked for death. Other gangs that have been marked for death with a green tag, like the Eighteen Street Gang (18th) and the Mara Salva Thrucha (MS 13), stood up to the Mexican Mafia and showed that they could control the war: a position that the Mexican Mafia saw as dangerous to their rule, so, in turn, the gangs that have pushed back eventually are given more say in the political structure of the Mexican Mafia.

Brick continued, giving me a rundown of the Asian Gang structure, and how a drawn-out war between the SS and the Asian Boyz (ABZ) and the Tiny Rascal Gang (TRG) has made it so that at different times the Asians have had to be housed in their own cellblocks, as jail administrators recognized that they didn't have the numbers to engage in the war.

The Long Beach sect of TRG have been engaged in a heated war with the Long Beach Southern Gangs, like the Longo 13, dating back to the early nineties. TRG affiliates in the San Fernando and San Gabriel Valley have taken up the call to war against any SS gang that shares their city space.

The Long Beach TRGs has maintained an allegiance with the Long Beach Crip Gangs (the Insane Crips and the Long Beach 20s) an alliance that has made for other Asian gangs to align with Bloods and Crips. The street alliance has made it possible for Asians to associate with African Americans. The rationale of "the enemy of my enemy is my friend" has proven to be the best course of action for both sides.

Caucasian inmates and unaffiliated Hispanics in LA County Jail are forced to align with the SS and have become the recipients of all the rules that the SS gang places on its members. Any citizen of the city who had one too many traffic tickets or a DUI arrest would be forced to fall in line or face death from the hands of his brethren. Their only other option is to seek help from the authorities, which then relegates them to a Special Needs Yard (SNY), commonly known as "PC" or Protective Custody.

The Pisanos, or Border Brothers as they affectionately refer to themselves, are made up of illegal immigrants from Mexico, and they have little interest in the gang wars they are captive to, but they walk the line in silence. Pieces of this convoluted gang system were given to me over the hours by Brick. I was able to discern how aligned Brick was with this way of life as he tossed around the words "Wetbacks," "Hat-dancers," and "Bean-eaters" with reckless abandon. But I would see that the gangster Hispanics used the same terms to describe an illegal, a Paisa (no), a group that the Mexican gangbangers believed were lower than them.

The gangster Hispanics would go through a series of call-and-response lines. They had a rehearsed line that would begin with one announcer shouting, "*Buenos dias!*" and with little dead air, the entire Hispanic population replied, "*Buenos dias!*" This would be the first of many calls that the SS would perform throughout the day. I had no issue sleeping through the drills. My SS cellmates didn't disturb me as they conducted business with neighboring cells— deals to trade bologna sandwiches for cookies or for the next day's bologna were conducted as the corrections officers (COs) served the morning meal.

I awoke at different stages of the day's activities: the COs served the meals with the same level of hate for the process as the inmates had for what we would have to consume. My cellmates had fashioned a makeshift curtain for privacy when one would sit at the toilet. The monotony of the day was interrupted when Brick and one of the SS jockeyed for position as they tried to catch a mouse that darted into our cell. Brick called the mouse Freeway Freddy and said that the COs had a bounty on the mouse, and whoever caught him could redeem his body for a burger.

Neighbors

"If I ran the zoo…" —Dr. Seuss

THE CHATTER ON THE tier came to an end with the clink-clank sound of metal hitting the concrete floor. Time froze as everyone on the tier waited for their leaders to explain where the sound had come from and what to do next. The seconds dragged on and the silence only served to allow for heartbeats to be heard through one's ears. Then a raspy voice spoke from the opposite end of the tier, "Aye, Cuz, what's up with that?"

Another voice served as reverb, "I'm on it."

Brick and the other two soldiers stood at attention in the cramped cell. One of the SS inmates had transferred out of the cell, leaving his comrade alone, sitting on the bunk with a vacant stare, looking the part of the condemned man, awaiting a last-minute reprieve.

A spokesman for the SS broke the silence with a statement in the Spanglish vernacular, "*Oyez mi gente*, and to the rest of the tier, we apologize for the disruption and everything is copacetic. *Homies, listo*, and *gracias!*"

His consoling statement was followed by a voice that rang out with authority, "Ay, everything is all good." Then, the sound of a toilet flush wrecked the silence. I reasoned from the Patois, and the timing of the last person, that it was a representative for the Africans that agreed that all would return to the level of calm that had been present before the metal clinking sound sent all into war mode.

Without any delay, Brick returned to a diatribe of how his lowrider compared to all others that cruised Crenshaw Boulevard. He simulated the flicking of car hydraulic turns by positioning himself in a squat as he "hit a switch" to "pancake" his lowrider to the ground. He jerked his body, rising as he hit the switch to bring his make-believe car back to its original position. Brick continued his story, and the normal chatter on the tier had resumed.

Later in the evening, Brick would tell me why the silence took place and why all went back to "normal." As he said in a direct manner, "Ma'fuckas know who holding a piece. You get caught slipping then it's my business." Everyone operates under the assumption that the opposition has stockpiled weapons. But, once a weapon is introduced—in order to maintain the status of force—the side that possess the weapon will dispose of the item to prove that the known threat has been eliminated.

I had grown annoyed with the sound of Brick's voice. I eagerly waited for the daily counts and for the COs to make announcements on the loudspeaker, knowing that Brick would then have to pause whatever tale he was in the middle of telling. I would get my reprieve, but it would come with my name being called so that I could take the journey to the satellite jail in Saugus, the Wayside facility.

The speaker rambled on with the list of names and cells for the nightly transfer and followed the list with the familiar command, "Get your shit ready. Your cells will crack in two minutes." Considering that I had little personal property, I gathered the indigent supplies provided upon entering the facility as Brick continued to advising me of what to be prepared for. I said my greetings and waited for the cell door to open. I wasn't sure why I was so eager to move around. I made the mistake of viewing movement as making progress that would relieve me of this world. I was just going to get a different view of this hellish world, not relief from it.

I studied the grease-stained bars and figured it best not to touch them with my bare hands. While looking at the layers of food and blood that had been painted over, Brick continued giving advice. "Get used to this. The shit shuffle is what they do, especially in county. Soon as you get settled, they gonna call your name at five in the morning to keep you off balance." I had little to add to Brick's statement. I thought, but didn't say, that I hoped I wouldn't be around long enough to withstand too many living adjustments.

The cell door opened and I emerged for the first time in days. Several other inmates on the tier stepped out and filed down the hall. As expected, every person in line would be required to recite their names and booking numbers at every checkpoint. The process to become an inmate was a laborious task, but the process to be transferred out of the county jail proved to serve up its own challenges. On my walk out of the housing unit, I studied the halls that made up a vast network of passageways. Several cellblocks came into view, and when I considered the maze of cellblocks that I had just walked through, I knew that the doors that I passed led to endless hallways.

If Seneca was right, and man is a reasoning animal, then all I'd have to do to stay out of the officer's way was follow instructions. Just follow the line without deviation. There was nothing about right or wrong or how the just world operated. No room for abstract thinking. I'd seen enough to know that this was an inhumane place, but if I adopted the character of an obedient follower of instructions, it was likely that I would make it through this hell without confrontation. At least, that was the plan.

There was an equal number of black and brown faces in this line formation. All appeared suspect of the person in line behind them— the hunched shoulders served to protect one's chin if attacked from the rear. We walked in silence, passing walls with western battle scenes. I wasn't able to view the artistry fully in the seconds that I passed, and for those that dared, the CO at the checkpoint reminded the group to "Keep fucking moving!"

This blue jumpsuit uniform that I had been assigned only served to enhance a pregnant boxy silhouette. Normally my athletic frame would be enhanced with the clothes that I wore, but now I appeared like a street urchin draped in tattered shreds. I negotiated my steps carefully so I wouldn't stumble. This jumpsuit had become the allegorical ball and chain that would thwart any attempt to escape. I was in a constant battle with pulling up my pants and keeping my hands behind my back, as ordered—this would not be easy.

An awaiting officer stopped my line and we were counted and directed to an open cell. We left our living units before the dinner meal, so I reasoned that it was before 6:00 p.m. My stomach had started cramping, and water alone would not satisfy the emptiness. I sat and waited along with everyone else for food that we knew would not come.

A passing female CO kindly relayed the time to the cell. Her big brown eyes and tiny heart-shaped mouth would stay with me for the remainder of the night, but it would do nothing to satisfy the pit in my stomach.

Neighboring cells held inmates in various stages of the release process; some were going to state prison, some were being released to other agencies, and some inmates were fortunate enough to be preparing for release back into society. I looked on as the inmates slated for release were given bags containing their personal belongings. I would've expected ecstasy from the newly freed men, but some of their faces spoke of the careful way that one has to accept good news when surrounded by other people that have a road of bad news ahead.

Without any clocks on the wall, I guessed that an hour had passed from the last update. We had been passed up for the nightly meal and it was obvious that we shouldn't expect food until the morning. (This was purgatory.) The occupants of the cell and all the neighboring cells screamed out for food, for transfer, for some kind of attention. The COs ignored every scream. Some of the cries sounded like a group of animals being tortured. Some of the screams were the result of hunger cramps—that was the pain I was experiencing.

A group of inmates stood at the window and watched a mouse in the hall run in and out of the various doors that lined the hall. Once the rodent found an exit, we were left to entertain ourselves.

The two hip-hop poets in the cell began a volley of insult rhymes that would now serve as our entertainment. I tried not to care much about the poets, but I would soon find myself enjoying the entertainment. Early in the battle there wasn't a hint of contempt for women or the system, but as the rhyming continued the taunting turned provocative, which challenged the opposition to create metaphors that wowed the crowd and the occasional passing CO. They were in full battle mode.

The Hispanic gangsters cheered as the once-friendly battle took on the topic of the illicit trade of drugs, sprinkled with talk of women and fast cars. I began to visualize the scenes and was anxious to see the next world that they would take us into. As they exchanged insults, the intensity grew and the potential for violence became cinematic. They spoke of the world they lived or wanted to live.

Before there could be any violence, each combatant calmed and extended their respect for the other with an embrace. The rhyming became a comfort for the cell, but the verbal battling gave way to the rattling of the chains in the hallway, and everyone prepped for transport.

Inmates scrambled to gather personal belongings. The faces of my captivated cellmates were now the faces of attentive travelers awaiting their boarding passes. Initially I didn't know why I was at attention, but it seemed proper to stand and wait for the next order, just as everyone else did.

The silence in the cell became a calling for one to stand alert and wait for the next command. My name was called early in the process and I was hooked to a four-man chain. We followed the pact as directed. The familiar threats rang out, "Shut the fuck up or I will cancel this fucking movement!"

We were told to sit and remain silent. The drive got underway and the music that played switched from hip-hop to Mexican Ranchero music. The SS didn't conceal their pleasure with the staff's selection, and in short order the black faces on the bus voiced their displeasure, but the officers showed no concern for dividing the music stations. It was becoming clear that the race relations were soiled, and the taunting by the officers showed that the problem went beyond the gang wars in the inner city. The childish actions of the officers were evidence that the sheriff deputies were not only encouraging the animosity but were a part of it. I began to wonder how far they would go in participating, if the opportunity were presented.

I understood basic Spanish and could make out what the officers were saying to the inmates in the seats near me. It was relayed that the Wayside facility we were headed to had just had riots, and as he said, "Miates" were the majority. He used the word Miate with an ease that relayed to the SS that he was one of them in word and action.

The roaring of the antique engine drowned out the full conversation, but I could see that the SS were underway with their planning. The little ant-faced officer was emboldened and filled with joy as he conversed with the SS. There was a dimension to this system I still didn't fully understand, so I sat and feigned ignorance to what I had heard. I was on a chain with three SS who beamed with pride of their momentary allegiance with the officers, black faces looked on, keenly aware of the animus surrounding us that fueled the gang wars in the county jail.

The steady humming of the engine had everyone nodding off to sleep. Slumber had overtaken us all, leaving one or two throughout the bus awake with the transporters. There would be little I could do if violence erupted while on the bus. I had one arm chained to the four-man restraint system. The cramped seating is purposely compacted as to deny its occupants leverage, nullifying any advantage for an attacker. I guessed that it was between two and four in the morning. I lost track of the day, and date. All I could see was the familiar I-5 North sign as the bus lumbered toward the Wayside facility. The head bobbing was evidence that rest was all that was on the minds of everyone, and without official approval, I joined the group and feigned sleep.

I'd mentioned to L that I never dreamed while asleep, that I reserved sleep for just that. I preferred to be in control, and that extended to my dreams as well. Now, as my head nodded from side to side, I ran through several versions of the stories I would tell my father. I didn't worry about what my mother would think because in her eyes I could do no wrong—it was my father's judgment that worried me. And I say my father, but he is really my grandfather, Walter. He adopted me as a child and raised me when my father, his son, abandoned his responsibilities. He was the man I had always worked to impress, and I knew that once he heard about my incarceration, he would abandon me too.

The ride came to an end at the Wayside complex, which housed thousands of LA County Jail inmates. The bus cleared several security checks, which slowed our entry. The transportation officers secured their weapons in the armory at one checkpoint and then we were allowed to continue on. The bus pulled into several gates before stopping where all inmates were herded off down a narrow hallway, through a labyrinth of turns, checks and rechecks of names and booking numbers, through another corridor in a single file line, finally emerging into an icebox-cold gymnasium for yet another full-body exam.

This was the second cavity check of the night, and this set of officers appeared energized when they got to the stage of the search where we had to bend over at the waist with our insides displayed. The sadist officer screamed out: "Re-grip your ass!" because he wasn't satisfied with how one inmate was holding his buttocks. "Cough, c'mon, everyone at once. If you fuck up we can be here all night." In order to blend in, I acquiesced to the homoerotic demand and re-gripped. Thankfully I was born with the gift of laughter and re-gripping wasn't a hassle in that moment. For the first time, these cavity searches gave me a laugh. Because of my regard for self,

I didn't dare laugh out loud, or at an audible tone, because I would hate to extend an invitation to the group of hyper-violent officers who assembled for the viewing of the anuses. I laughed without anyone knowing. I doubt if anyone cared. I was resigned to my world, in a gymnasium with over one hundred men in an extremely emasculating position for far too long, all for the officers to maintain the safety and security of the institution—my laughter continued.

Whatever someone may be hiding in their anal cavity, they must really want it. He would've worked hard for it, and if the contraband that he was hiding fell out during the search, which officer would be charged with collecting the evidence?

Someone passed gas and the room tried to hold back laughs and failed. Passing gas was the one thing that bound cops and robbers. A natural discharge brought everyone back to a level playing field. Laughter followed as natural as the gas that no one claimed responsibility for. "Shut the fuck up! I'll have you motherfuckers sitting here all night. You think that's funny?" There was one officer who didn't share in the bond formed by the release of the methane joke.

We finished the search without any further incident and my line walked on while an officer stood with his pepper-ball gun trained on the movement. We collected our blue jumpsuits and bedding under the threat of harm if we slowed the process. "No one fucking look this way!" the officer screamed. Names and booking numbers were read and once again we shuffled off to our designated units.

My group entered the dorm and I paused at the nauseating scent that filled the unit. It was early morning and entirely dark, save the dimmed night-lights. The dorm was appropriately muted. A clock was affixed to the wall, and the moving hands highlighted how long I had gone since last eating. I didn't know how long I had to sleep before the dormitory would be filled with movement. I was disgusted at the idea of being crammed into a dorm with over 150 inmates in beds stacked like coffins, three levels high. The bottom bunk had a foot of clearance off the ground, with another two feet of space before the middle bunk began; the occupant of the middle bunk had the same two feet before he was entombed by the third bunk, which was the only one without a lid, giving it five feet of overhead. My thoughts went to how much more care goes into burying the deceased than what has been extended to the living.

The feeling that I was entering the ancient catacombs filled my mind. Some men were awaiting trials; some serving out jail sentences for any range of violations; and from the looks of the transient pacing the floor, some didn't know what they were doing here with the condemned.

I made my way into a brightly lit bathroom, followed quickly by the transient inmate nervously pulling at his tussled hair, which looked to be the beginning of dreadlocks. He surveyed the group of new arrivals, and in the same nervous fashion that he entered the room, he left. I searched the bedding that I was provided and quickly retrieved socks and underpants.

The officer closed the grill gate after the last inmate entered, not showing much care for those that slept. Once again, the transient appeared and disappeared in the room with vole-like speed, not pausing long enough to say anything remotely comprehensible.

The representatives for the SS gang approached the Mexican inmates, inquiring about their gang affiliations and their respective criminal charges. I listened as he spoke about their laws, or as he referred to them, *reglas*. The representative turned his attention to me, asking if I was an SS.

My quick reply was delivered in a measured tone, without a trace of fright or contempt for his gang, "No, *soy Cubano*."

His next question was the defining moment that would dictate our current and future interactions. "Who do you run with?"

The group I ran with or the gang I may be affiliated with would be of more importance than my ethnic makeup. "I'm with the Others," I replied, continuing to pull up my socks.

"*Listo. Oyez Cubano…*" He rambled on into his greetings and introduced himself as Tricky from El Monte, then respectfully excused himself, giving his attention to his new recruits.

Within seconds of me declaring my affiliation, the representative for the Brothers entered the picture and introduced himself as Biggie from East Coast Crip. I assumed the transient was a scout and reported to Biggie that I may be affiliated with their side. Biggie told me to rest for the next two hours and that he would give me the "rundown" once everyone was up. I took Biggie up on his offer and made my way to my assigned bunk at the far end of the dorm.

Biggie stood at least six foot three and weighed upward of two fifty. He claimed to be from the same gang as Brick, and so it seemed apparent that the East Coast Gang was represented entirely by giants. Biggie walked with me to my bunk and in a low tone gave the basic rules. His Southern drawl made it a struggle for me to understand clearly what he was saying. The part of his talk that was clear was that the representative for the "Africans" was asleep and that he and other soldiers were on guard. Knowing that Biggie was on guard was reassuring. He had an aureole of electrified hair that gave him the look of someone plucked from the 1970s. Each step he took sounded like he was creating cracks in the concrete floor. I took comfort as he stood by while I made my bed.

Brick's knowledge of the gang world had gained traction as I surveyed the dorm and reviewed my bus ride to this facility. It had become clear that the seriousness of this war that the SS and the Bloods and Crips were engaged in on the streets of LA took its orders from the prison gangs. I had to devise a plan on how I would survive this world. But, for now, I decided to do battle with sleep, and without wasting time, I slid into the middle bunk.

"*Reveille. Reveille. Reveille…*Wake up!" the speakers blasted. It sounded as if the Rough Riders had stormed the dorm, as the trumpets wailed, awakening me from sleep. I expected to see soldiers running around the periphery of the Alamo, but I wasn't in a western dream.

This was the dorm's wakeup call, and without much rush, inmates started to file into lines for sinks and toilets. Some had already prepared for the day. The majority walked in a daze with heavy-lidded eyes.

The cramped bathroom was no larger than a one-car garage outfitted with two trough-style washbasins on either side of a raised island. Across from the basin was the communal trough for urinating. Two toilets sat next to the trough and without much direction anyone could deduce that the toilets closest to the trough were for relieving oneself while standing up. The toilet next to the standup toilet was off-limits, giving anyone that would be sitting down for relief at the last three toilets a buffer zone from the possibility of splashing urine.

Biggie pulled me aside as I waited for my turn at the basin. He would give me a thorough understanding of the house rules and then he provided me with a care package that contained a tube of toothpaste and a bar of soap. Before I could inquire about the overture, Biggie assured me that the gratuity was from the community pot that the Brothers contribute to.

The lines moved with assembly line precision, the flow of tattooed bodies moving in time. I studied the intricate artwork on the arms and backs of my new neighbors. Street corners that represented their affiliations were emblazoned on necks and faces, leaving little room to distinguish the individual from a graffiti-stained wall. Many of the tattooed SS that marked their faces showed no regard for the disfiguring permanence that a black-shaded "18" would have on their lives. I managed not to stare, but even at a distance, the numbers were clearly visible.

In an accent and with a pitch that was interestingly foreign, Biggie pointed to where the Brothers and Others sat to eat. I surveyed the room and imagined what Biggie might've been talking about. I could see that the dayroom tables transformed into the eating area daily at the three meal servings, and without surprise, the eating area was segregated.

Filling the role of town jester, the old transient that roamed the dorm when I arrived would stand at the front of the dorm staring at the female officer on the other side of the grilled gate. He made the squeezing motion as if he were enjoying ripe melons, all while the officer conversed with a male officer, who would work hard to hold in his laughs. "Stupid ass DTG!" is what a young Crip would say as he laughed while walking into the bathroom. (The transient embraced the title DTG: Downtown Gangsta.) The laughter spread, causing the officer to turn, only to find that the DTG had begun to wave his hands like a wild conductor, defusing the officer, never giving her an idea that she was the subject of the laughter.

Two boiled eggs, two pieces of white bread, one cup of cold cereal, and a child-sized milk and orange juice served as the morning meal. Without much contemplation or attempt to add spices to the bland taste, I devoured the meal. I would rush to take in tap water, so I could wash down the bread that was lodged in my throat. I could smell the coffee that was prepared by some inmates, along with various commissary items in an attempt to bring the meal to a state that resembled a proper café-style meal.

Biggie appeared like a guardian, advising me that I could lie down until the dorm's final wakeup call at 9:00 a.m. Before I left the bathroom, I would be introduced to the representative for the Brothers. Joe was a short rotund man with a smooth black bald head. He stood in front of me, but his eyes continued to survey the room. I still didn't feel a part of the world I was a captive in.

A meeting was about to begin with Biggie and Joe, so without delay, I made my way to my bunk. On the walk, I noticed that the *Los Angeles Times* was provided to the dorm. I thumbed through the obituary section looking for a familiar name, scanning and rescanning, desperately hoping to read my accuser's name. His death would provide me with a reprieve from this hell that I was enduring.

In my youth, I had a habit of counting the number of times that I would chew my food on either side of my mouth. I used the lines in my fingers that defined my joints as markers for my incessant calculations. Cracks in walkways and brick walls provided me endless entertainment where I could add, subtract, and eventually start a new pattern, contingent on the number I ended with being a prime number.

This bean-counting routine began in reform school, and I continued it as a way to assert a semblance of control in a world where I had very little. Just as I was currently under the control of the LA sheriffs as a juvenile delinquent, I had been made a ward of the court and my every move was dictated by sadistic guardians, most being Vietnam veterans who had never relieved themselves of the thirst for the sight of blood.

Prime number calculations were my one mental outlet that was beyond censorship by my captors then, and as I stared at the grated gates that separated the inmates from the sheriffs, endless calculations began to present themselves. The problem that I had as a youth would undoubtedly plague my mind this tour as well. Where I had started the number-crunching as a way to escape from my physical confines, I eventually became lost in numbers. But, I had a plan this time—or so I thought—and would only allow myself to indulge in counting routines when on my bunk. I would need to be keenly aware of everyone in my space. There could be no room for error. I had imaginary enemies who wielded real weapons and could alter my world forever.

Play Time
The Yard

"The most pitiful thing in the world is a mob...
They don't fight with the courage they're born with.
They fight with courage borrowed from their numbers."
—Mark Twain, *The Adventures of Huckleberry Finn*

THROUGH MY FAINT SNORING I could hear the officer barking orders on the loudspeaker. "Get ready for yard! Anybody late is going to the fucking hole! Get your fucking asses up!"

I had been in Wayside for two days and all I desired was sleep. I didn't remember what had been served for the night meal or if I had awoken to retrieve it. In those two days I managed to sleep through the SS administering corporal punishment to one of their comrades ("discipline" as they call it). Some unfortunate character had been accused of a violation of the group rules and was unable to sway the politicians to his side of the argument. They reasoned that without the punishment, the other groups would perceive them as weak. So, a public beating was the prescribed sentence, so all could see and take notice of what could be if they violate the *reglas*.

During my time in the back of the dormitory, I constantly overheard heretical conversations from several of the SS. With so many of the SS members sharing the same grievances, it would eventually cause their structure to crumble on itself. The low threshold of proof needed to convict weighed on their minds, a fact made obvious as the chatter would die down as certain leaders in the group appeared. The penalty for treason would be met with death; as it stood, SS were being disciplined for imaginary crimes, as the charges defied definition altogether. Group mentality was the norm in this hell.

My line formation position in front of Biggie was not by design, but I took comfort in the safety of his influence. I watched how the various groups chose their placement in line. The rival groups work to avoid being placed next to a hostile. But there are only so many places one can assume in a single file line, and at some point someone runs out of options and all that will serve as a defense when your back is to an enemy is to assume the defensive posture and roll your shoulders forward to create a hunch to the back, as you attempt to guard the jugular.

The line movement traversed the neighboring dorms, allowing split-second interactions with the inmates housed inside. The brief encounter allowed for many to communicate with quick hand signs. Some displayed their gangs with rapid finger movements, relaying full messages in the few seconds of interaction.

Officers were posted in teams of two. Some gripped their flashlights like batons and the officers seemed all too eager to adjust the cranial structure of an inmate. Several of the officers had electrified Taser guns. Everything about this experience to me resembled the footage on the nightly news of a war-torn country. I knew I wanted to escape, but after seeing the security detail that was deployed to allow our unit to visit the recreation yard, my thoughts of running for freedom subsided. They invited anyone to test their security.

The words "recreation yard" loosely described the slab of concrete we were allowed to use for exercise. Concertina wire encased the single basketball court. The rusted rims didn't have nets, or lines marking the outlines. Black and brown inmates divided the court in half. A sitting area was provided with five tables in a cluster, under a decrepit wooden awning. The division of the yard mirrored the splitting of real estate in the dorm. It had become clear that the side I chose to align with would determine every part of my life in this hell.

The cramped concrete yard had grown crowded as another dorm joined. I had believed that I had a fix on the makeup of the various characters that I shared living space with, but these unfamiliar faces changed the chemistry of the scene in a predatory way. I retreated to a parcel of concrete that was for neither black nor brown, but a thoroughfare of sorts for anyone that wanted travel. I believed it to be the one way that I could send a message that I was not involved in their war.

I saw a familiar face as the yard continued to fill beyond its intended capacity. I waited for him as he engaged in his obligatory greetings. I remembered that he was affiliated with the Bloods. I knew that he held a respectable rank in his fraternity, so I reasoned that having an association with him could be beneficial. Snoop is the name I remembered. Calling his name would draw the attention of the officers, so instead I decided to wave his attention to me.

Snoop's broad African face was what you would expect to see of a tribesman from the Congo. It was a face with a strong forehead and a thick nose that had been mashed flat. As he approached I could see his eyes darting from my hands to my face. He maintained awareness of the yard as he walked toward me, stepping with an effortless swing, never allowing his face to betray his true emotion. I was relieved that he recognized me, and without a pause in flow, we greeted with a standard fist bump and a half-hearted hug.

Snoop and I exchanged stories during the booking stage of my ordeal. The ease that he had in adjusting to this society was evidence that he had accepted the inhumane treatment that started with the three-day booking and the racial tension as a natural part of the gang life.

Snoop positioned himself so that he had an unobstructed view of the yard. His posturing made it clear to anyone who might consider an attack that he wouldn't go down easily. I assumed the same state of alert as Snoop exchanged greetings with members of his Blood crew. The greetings that were extended to Snoop were passed on to me. Having audience with Snoop allowed me a view of the coordinated security squad that the Brothers devised that was made up of both Bloods and Crips.

To an onlooker, the actual topic of Snoop's conversation was hidden as he talked while pretending to be in the midst of a hip-hop recital. He lightly pounded his chest with a clenched fist, which served to create the bass line for his imaginary rap. His mask was complete as I caught on to his tactics by rocking my head to show that I was enjoying his lyrics. In place of the pimp culture that is often depicted in hip-hop lyrics, Snoop used his mask to make me aware of what was soon to unfold on the yard. With no immediacy to his voice, and staying on the beat, Snoop began to tell me who was about to be disciplined.

The SS gang was prepping the yard's rival crews for their discipline session. Snoop said the news from the SS served two purposes: On one end it was a sign of respect, and it also warned anyone not involved to secure their soldiers so that they wouldn't react, believing that one of their soldiers was at the bottom of the pack. Snoop would take pleasure in the attack that was set to take place. He found it hilarious, that everyone knew what was about to happen except the one due to get attacked.

While we awaited the attack from the SS on one of their own, Snoop revealed that the SS had a mission to take control over certain neighborhoods, to monopolize the drug trade. Like most people not affected by this war that Snoop spoke of, I was shocked. Snoop emphasized that there was a full war with SS underway in LA over failed drug trades and that like any power grab, there was going to be collateral damage, which often affects the innocent. Snoop saw that the SS goal was being paved with "dead black faces that were not a part of the gang war" and took issue with what he said was the indiscriminate targeting of anyone with black skin in the contested neighborhoods. His anger quickly turned to the Mexican Mafia—they were the ones who set the mandate from the inside that the SS are carrying out.

After listening to the chronicles of war, I realized that the part of town that is under prison mandates was less than five miles from my home and the gated communities of Beverly Hills. The five miles could've been a thousand, because in my neighborhood, I was unaffected by the street-level drug wars. We shared the same city in name only.

I asked Snoop what was the goal of these terrorists? In a tone that was dead to sentiment, Snoop carried on with what I can describe as a fairy tale, in that the SS goal was to "take over California." Had there been a hint of jest I would've laughed to break the heavy conversation, but there was none. Snoop went on telling me how SS are using their ill-gotten gains to purchase real estate in the neighborhoods in an attempt to physically own a street.

Snoop would point to the SS embrace of the hip-hop culture and all the trappings of wealth—gold chains and luxury cars—as evidence of their success in the drug trade. He was deathly convinced they could accomplish their goals. The same geographical barriers that allowed me to exist in my part of town without being affected by the drug wars also existed in the inner city. The barriers that bound them to their side of town also served to cloud their sense of logic. Even Don Quixote would've understood that in a modern society, like California, it would be impossible for a criminal enterprise to accomplish such an endeavor. As improbable as the notion may be, according to Snoop, they intended to "take over California," or, as he corrected himself, "take back California!"

Had I engaged Snoop into further dialogue and presented a counterargument to his understanding of the SS goals to "take over" California, it would've fallen on deaf ears. All he saw was the evidence on the ground, in the form of gold chains and luxury cars. I knew that I was engaged in a society that had illusions of grandeur that were removed from reality. I quickly found it in my best interest to reserve my judgment.

Snoop never took an eye off the yard. Our conversation came to a close when two SS unleashed a flurry of punches on the marked man. I followed Snoop's lead as he made his way to the far side of the yard where all the Brothers congregated. As we walked, I eyed the fence, flirting with the notion of an escape. My soul wanted out, but I knew better already than to display any outward sign of that.

The two attackers failed to put down the marked man with their initial shots. Surprisingly, he shook off their heavy blows and managed to remain upright. Once he broke free, he raised his hands to protect his face without blocking his line of sight. Turning on his lead foot—solidifying his orthodox fighting stance, left foot forward, left shoulder toward his two opponents—he made the attempt to battle.

The officers looked on without any sense of immediacy. Just when the victim appeared to be able to handle the inital attack, two more soldiers joined the fight and the marked man's defense was overtaken. It was possible that he remained upright by the competing shots that were delivered from his front and back. He wouldn't last much longer.

Time may have been delayed for me, but I imagine the time vacuum that the marked man was caught in lingered, only stopping and restarting as each shot landed. Eventually, the cavalry arrived, with upward of twenty officers storming the yard with staff clubs in hand, screaming for everyone to lie facedown on the ground. Snoop had the presence of mind to deliver a joke, mocking the officers' arrival with a line that was all too appropriate: "The bulls are coming! The bulls are coming!"

We would lie facedown for over an hour as the sheriffs' investigative staff processed the crime scene, photographing and cataloging the assailants. Any Mexican in the vicinity of the assault would be subjected to a more thorough review, as the officers proceeded with the dragnet approach to the investigation; lock it down and sort it out later was the protocol.

Before the investigators closed the scene, they demanded that the entire yard be subjected to a body scan. Any bruising of the knuckles would be an indicator of one having been involved in a fight. I reviewed my knuckles, hoping that they weren't discolored from my constant fist clenching. I couldn't worry about what wasn't under my control. I could only think of the hate I had for this hell.

When the marked man passed on the gurney, I was able to discern that he had sustained puncture wounds to his upper body. He may not have noticed the wounds himself as his adrenaline jumpstarted his instincts into survival mode. The marked man appeared fully alert, so it was doubtful that he would succumb to his wounds.

The sheriffs' tactical teams' militaristic response to the incident should've been enough for Snoop to review his assessment of the SS goal of "taking back California," as the sheriffs left little room for anyone to question who would remain in control if such an attempt were made.

SNOOP ADVISED ME TO keep my eyes open for any time that the SS gained an advantage in population because that's when they always struck out—whether at their own or against the Brothas. As we stood to exit the yard, Snoop rambled on. He didn't fear reprisal from the officers, who were focused on the SS that remained in the prone position. "Now the bulls will move about ten more of these hat dancers into my dorm and we gonna see how they puff up their chests."

Under my breath and out of the side of my mouth, I asked, "How often do you get moved?"

Snoop showed less concern for concealing his statement. "You gonna always be the new motherfucker to the unit. They want to keep you off balance, but they always make sure that the SS can have the numbers."

The nauseating scent of the dormitory lingered night and day. Every morning was met with the annoyingly loud call, "Reveille, Reveille, Reveille," and as the morning dragged on I would be pestered by an even more irritating call that would ring out from the mouth of the designated SS crier: "*Buenos dias*, homies!" The crying went on without a second of dead air from the foot soldiers as they replied with as much false bravado as they had the day before, "*Buenos Dias!*" I tried to close my ears as the crier carried on with his obsessive ceremonial speech replete with jingoistic pomp. The whole affair had become uncomfortable.

The SS were the schoolyard bullies. Anyone experienced with bullies could recognize that the SS display of unity was more rooted in insecurity than in strength. I am conflicted for whom I have compassion for: the dissenters of the ceremony who secretly protest in their hearts, or the ones that blindly participate with a weird adolescent devotion, as if there is a paradise waiting at the end of their service to the cause.

The marathon booking process had proven a physically draining task and I had yet to reset my circadian rhythm. I had been incarcerated for two weeks, and each day I scanned the obituary section of the paper, and each day I grew more and more disappointed at the name I didn't see amongst the departed.

The sun had yet to break through the holes in the grated screens covering the windows. No calls of Reveille had rung out yet. I was anticipating this day; because I had court scheduled. My nervous energy had built up to the point where sleep had become less spontaneous. I was unable to establish any pattern that could be considered normal. I walked the dorm when I should've been asleep. I slept when I should've been awake, interacting with my new neighbors.

I waited for the call to file out for court. The DTG crisscrossed the dorm at full attention, patrolling as a self-appointed civil servant, his fragility tied to his survival. The inmates that mocked his behavior and decrepit frame didn't recognize the strength he displayed in unplugging from the expected hardened convict character. His comedy made clear that he was not a threat. Daily he walked amongst all groups and pleaded for various items that he consistently received. This was his world, and everyone else was merely a visitor in it.

The preacher of the unit was awake, conducting a group in prayer. During his speeches, the preacher never spoke of his personal trials, and instead he focused on the problems that other people faced and took someone else's ordeal to peddle his form of spiritual guidance. He was a prophet to some, a soothsayer of sorts, and as the followers left his group with a renewed sense of energy, his reputation grew and the words he spoke began to carry weight. The preacher's low register required those that gathered to lower their heads and listen to every word individually: "The reality of a future without hope is too overbearing. Hope will have to be our world entirely."

The majority of the SS refused religious guidance. I reasoned that if they would experience an awakening of the religious kind, then they would wrestle with what they know to be the proper approach to scripture, and they would be left with clear options: stay in the gang and deny what they know to be true, or fully convert and face persecution for their beliefs.

The preacher closed his blessings and ended with, "God exists in your search for him." The two inmates who awaited transport to court with me sat in silence, clenching their Bibles. The penitents carried out intricate superstitious movements once called to report to the grilled gate, as a sign that their journey would be blessed. I followed the groups as they walked with a swing to their walk, as if they had become full of some spiritual juice that would allow them to face their obstacles. Before the court movement could exit, we were pushed aside as the SS that withstood the discipline beating the night before seized the opportunity to escape the dorm.

He shuffled forward, revealing his swollen face to the officers, and was allowed to proceed to safety.

From a safe distance, my thoughts produced a string of primes: two guards with batons; three medical staff; five Southern Mexicans grouped across from me; twenty-three inmates on the basketball court. This was my new game and it might allow me to laugh at these bad actors and their pathetic plays.

Civil Order

Back to Court

"Listen! The court jester's cap and bells. The king is coming!"
—Ljupka Cvetanova

HAD MY NAME NOT been repeated so often, it would have been easy to pretend the court was discussing the fate of some other stranger that had mistakenly violated the laws of the land. Neither the clerks nor the stenographers nor the judge acknowledged my presence throughout the hearing. No one in the courtroom looked in my direction. The only eyes that acknowledged my presence were those of the sheriff assigned to the courtroom and my girlfriend, L, who sat in the audience, fighting back tears.

In order of severity, a woman in a frumpy pantsuit read the charges. The judge surveyed the courtroom, eventually locking eyes with my attorney, never turning his head to address me. My plea had been entered, "Not guilty." Still, no one acknowledged that I was in the room. And then I was ushered out of the courtroom by an aggressive sheriff. In the presence of the judge, the sheriff handled me with care and with a level of dignity that was notably absent once we returned to the holding cells.

An inmate was removed from the courtroom in handcuffs. He had played into the hand of the hyper-violent sheriff, who cranked the inmate's arms behind his back, lifting him off his feet. Another sheriff shouldered the inmate, snapping the inmate's shoulder. The inmate screamed, but no one stirred. He chose to challenge the authority of the officers and for that he was set straight as he adjusted to his new life as a cripple.

Minutes passed before an officer approached my cell. He buckled a devilish mask to his face and screamed orders for the cell to turn and face the wall. Everyone complied without protest, and then the cell door opened and the injured inmate was deposited. He worked hard to muffle his pain, but his shallow breathing gave way to a death scream that carried for several minutes. The cell door remained open as the sheriffs stood watch, waiting for anyone to challenge their authority.

The only redeeming act that came out of the inmate assault was in the compassion that my fellow inmates extended. Black and brown alike assisted in the best way that they could. One inmate fashioned a sling, attempting to stabilize the injured arm. I kept my distance, considering that the medical profession was never a passion of mine and I didn't want to draw the attention of the officers that I knew would be returning.

A group of officers arrived at the cell door. "I understand that someone fell," one of them said. It was a statement, not a question, and they were making it known that they were not going to accept a story that deviated from their official report about how the inmate fell, about how heroic the officers were in assisting him. He stated that what he said was official and without waiting for rebuttal, he backed his way out of the cell, allowing for the officers that stood on guard to extract the injured inmate from the cell with little care for his pain. A minute later, the cell I was in was cleared of all inmates, and we were divided between other holding cells while we awaited transport back to Wayside.

I was locked into a four-man chain and told to "Shut the fuck up" for the tenth time that day. I tried to process the seriousness of the court proceedings that I had just witnessed, but I couldn't stabilize my neck as the officer driving the bus rammed the accelerator as he bullied other drivers for rights to lanes. It was clear that this bullish approach was what they had been taught in their academy. The driver of the bus acted in the same fashion that the court officers did as they handled the assault of the inmate. I thought of how ironic it was that all of this crime was being perpetrated just across from the historic LA City Hall.

The Metro bus stops at the base of the steps sheltered several elderly Hispanic ladies with their sun-worn, leathery hands that clutched bags filled with bundles of produce and cleaning supplies. The ladies worked hard to ignore the bus as we waited at the red light. Other people at the stop lowered their heads as if they viewed our bus as a funeral procession. Several city dwellers holding signage, reminding passersby that "giving is the price you pay for your entrance to heaven." I laughed after reading the moral twist to the extortion tactics of shaming citizens into charity.

Longing for my former life choked me as tears began to fill my eyes. In an attempt to mask my pain, I rested my head against the seat in front of me, pretending that I was sleeping. When I finally looked back up, the entire bus had lowered their heads into the seats.

The entrance gates to the Wayside facility greeted the bus and quickly engulfed us into the compound. A phalanx of officers stood ready to receive the bus and process us through with the obligatory body search. Like an obedient exhibitionist, I lined up with the other inmates and submitted to the orders of: "Squat, cough, lift up your balls, roll your tongue, re-grip!"

The gang coordinator stood by scanning inmates' bodies as he looked for the meaning behind certain tattoos. Like everyone else in line, when he asked me the standard questions of my name and gang affiliation, I answered. I knew that there was a thin line between being direct and combative, and I studied how to best distinguish the two. I wouldn't be given the latitude to have a bad day. Any sign of aggression would be met with aggression, multiplied by the ten officers that stood waiting for the opportunity to test their newly acquired submission maneuvers. The short stocky officer who stood down the hallway was a familiar face—he worked nights at a club I used to frequent. Attempting to make contact would place the officer in a position to have to explain how or why he knew me, and considering we weren't exactly friends, I had no idea what topic of conversation I could even lead in with.

I arrived back to the dorm that I had left at 3:00 p.m. I hoped that I had missed the daily drama, but I knew that it would be prudent for me to familiarize myself with the day's activities, in the event that earlier dealings were still on the minds of someone who might want revenge. Instead of seeking out a briefing from Biggie, I opted to sleep. I wanted the escape that sleep would provide me. I was unable to devise a proper plan of how to physically escape, so the dream world would have to be my playground.

In the days that followed, I participated in the rituals of the dorm. I listened to the gang chants. I honored the Jim Crow-type rules that the SS had enacted. I checked incessantly the names in the obituary. I was most comfortable watching the operations of the dorm from my perch. Daily I wondered, what crimes had brought all these men here? My routine was simple: eat, shower, use the phone, and observe. Periodically I would have to entertain conversation from neighbors. I made it a habit not to become too invested in anyone's trials, and I knew not to inquire into someone's business dealings.

I had observed the structure of the SS organization. The leaders have their minions, bestowed the title of comrade or soldier, who do their bidding, mainly out of fear rather than a real belief in their way of life. The minions will never voice their dislike for the structure, but their hatred is visible in the less-than-exuberant response to the constant call-and-response drills. Their eye rolls and hissing breaths tell me all I need to know.

I observed the new arrival to the unit. The man had the look of a veteran, with his tough-guy confidence—the tattoos served as his calling card for anyone who may want to inquire about his affiliation. He exchanged handshakes with Biggie, who was providing the rules of the house—the same rules that I was given. The new arrival nodded and followed, and Brick rambled on. I hadn't been in Wayside long enough to be considered an expert on the complexities of the warring factions, but I knew that the tour by Brick was necessary. No matter how much of a veteran of the system you are, with the constant shuffling of inmates by the officers, at some point you will be the new guy and giving you the rules of the house is the obligation of someone like Biggie. Order is the objective and egos have to be sacrificed. Once given, it is on you to follow.

The minions' regard for self is what keeps them from making a stand against the group. The often trivial disciplining of their brethren is carried out in a ritualistic fashion: three soldiers surround the individual to be disciplined and exchange punches for thirteen seconds; the thirteen seconds is to honor the 13th letter of the alphabet: M. The frivolity in the charges serves as a warning of what could come to anyone who may try to have a position other than the unified position of the groups.

A minion with the SS gang would have to set aside his legal proceedings if the group demanded his service. Several times minions that had court scheduled the next day were called up to assist in punishing another minion who violated a rule. There was no regard for the individuals participating in a gang assault, who, if caught, would most certainly have another hurdle to overcome in the current case that he was being held on—in addition to the new assault charges for the discipline. The corporal discipline for the slightest offense ensured that the group would have a fear-unified, paramilitary squad that would be ready to deploy to any imaginary war without question—the effectiveness of the squad was not high on the list of priorities; showing up was their goal.

The days passed and I began to adopt certain aspects of my neighbor's program. The neighbor slept in the bottom bunk of the three-stack bed next to my rack. Kaos was his *nom de guerre*. He was a baby-faced kid who was being held to answer to two counts of first-degree murder. Often in our brief conversations the details of his life would dribble out. He carried photos of his girlfriend and closest buddies as reminders of the life he used to live. He imagined that if he carried the photos of loved ones that were engaged in living, in the wider world, then they would carry him out of this world.

I had received photos the night before from an ex-girlfriend and her dog. M had made the conscious decision to stay connected with me, as she knew that I faced an uncertain future. She made no attempt to rekindle a past love with retrospectives on what we had. I was blown away at how she focused on getting me to see a future aside from being a captive. I held the photos of M close, in the fashion that I had witnessed Kaos holding his. I didn't have any prescribed spells that would carry my desires, but the images of M provided the comfort that Kaos seemed to have after reviewing the life he sought to escape to.

Kaos worked holes in his shoes as he nervously moved about, preparing for his girlfriend's visit every weekend. He was awake early and wanted to talk, but all I wanted to do was return to sleep. I decided to be neighborly and to entertain Kaos. I would find, like everyone else, he was holding tight to a dilemma. He was a street artist, or as he called it, a tagger. And being Mexican, the SS demanded that he and other taggers pledge allegiance to their flag, or risk surviving alone as an enemy. He wasn't seeking my advice on the gang association, as he had already made his decision. He seemed to have little illusion as to what he was a part of and how life would play out for him. His hope was for a victory in the courtroom, and this is where he asked for my advice.

For reasons that I could not readily find, Kaos asked me what I would do if I had the opportunity, as he did, to turn evidence on someone in order to receive a more favorable sentence. Then it was clear. On one hand, I didn't want to dismiss Kaos's question as it showed that he trusted me, on the other hand, I didn't want to be overheard conspiring with Kaos as he plotted his life moving forward as an informant, or as this world called it, a rat.

I told him I didn't have that dilemma and hoped I never would. Kaos sensed that I didn't want to continue that line of conversation, and he quickly changed course. He was aware that he could be writing his own death sentence, so in a playful manner he added that he had a "homeboy" who had recently chosen that route, and that he could never be a rat. I knew that he was setting his defense in the event that I chose to inform his group that he would soon be a witness against his coconspirators. Kaos let the question die without receiving the blessing he hoped I would give.

On visiting days, Kaos would retrieve a set of freshly creased clothes that he had packed under his mattress. He was fastidious with the care that went into his appearance. His ritual included layering on globs of hair product to achieve the perfect coif hairstyle, like a 1950s schoolboy. He would recheck several times, ensuring that every hair follicle fell in line with the group. He worked hard at his look. Prior to Kaos choosing me to confide in, his conversations were a welcome moment of camaraderie, to break up the miserable reality of our existence. Now I had the burden of knowing who he was.

I prepared myself for the visit I was expecting. And when I was called before Kaos, he grew in agitation, as he considered how his girlfriend was usually the first person in the visiting room. Kaos wished me well and, without much thought, offered me a glob of hair gel.

As I hurried to get to the visiting area, I realized that it would serve me well to lower my expectations of what would be provided in the way of comfort. I walked on the painted lines that stretched the hall, leading me to the visiting room where a sheriff was positioned at the table, directing inmates where to report. I received my booth and worked at holding myself back from running to the next stage. On the walk I was able to look between the partitions and I was able to eye the visitors on the other end of the glass, but I was certain not to focus on anyone in particular as I arrived at my booth where I saw L, and my friend, Frankie. Their glued-on smiles were clearly a sign they had been briefed to remain cheerful upon receiving me.

L couldn't hold her excitement, launching into conversation before I could place the phone to my ear. I wanted to tell her to pause. She blinked, and a stream of tears fell down her face. She didn't fight the emotion any longer, which allowed the release of the well that she had stored. I could do nothing but watch and hope that she could control herself enough to have a conversation.

She eventually gained control and continued on, speaking quickly, her voice cracking as she worked to keep together. "Hey, babe!" was a comforting thing to hear. I would've been satisfied with hearing her say those words in a loop for the entire visit. The simplicity of the sound was comforting. Then I met her attempt at an embrace by placing my hands against the window. Oh, this ordeal was going to challenge my patience and any other virtue that may be summoned to deal with adversity. I knew at some point during the visit we would have to discuss the reason for our disgusting meeting: my confinement.

She rambled on with updates and well wishes from friends. I allowed myself a moment of laughter as I observed the trinkets and scarf she wore which seemed to be more poignant than practical. I took joy in imagining that she had worn all the items that I had ever given her, just to please me. I sat watching as she fidgeted with her accessories like a nervous schoolgirl. Her sensuous fingers traced hearts into the glass as she spoke. Frankie sat behind her, not saying much and eventually stepping away, affording us a bit of privacy.

I gave in to a comfort and began to catalogue seven seconds of silence from L after I said, "I love you."

I didn't know how much to reveal to L while using the prison phones that were being monitored and for the first half of the visit I decided to allow L to drive the conversation. She would immediately deliver me to a memory of a passionate experience we shared. L found a clever way to inject laughter into the visit, when she departed from the experience she was describing. She asked me if I had really been deprived of relations with a woman since my arrest. Her attempt at a joke was welcome, but it also got me thinking if I would ever be allowed to enjoy another sexual memory with L, or any woman—a concern I didn't dare voice.

L had other plans. Even in deplorable conditions like this visiting room, natural urges refused to die. Her juvenile sex talk had caused my spirit to reconstitute itself, awakening desires that until now were repressed. I didn't know where to focus my attention: her soft skin, her full lips, or that talented mouth—how will I keep her? I have nothing to offer to satisfy her sexual desires. My conversation can only do so much. I listened as she reminded me of how pleased I had made her in the past. But, that was the past. L worked herself down to three seconds of silence between my "I love you" and her jubilant proclamation of love for me.

Frankie returned and L passed him the phone. Slowly he sat in the chair that occupied the space at the booth. L's appearance in the background was washed away by Frankie's commanding frame. He had comprehensive knowledge of my legal case, which allowed him to speak candidly, providing his opinion as to how he thought I should proceed. He asked if "my cleaner would be able to wash a friend's house" and I knew what he was asking. He wanted to know if I had an asset in place to eliminate the one person that stood in the way of my having freedom. I paused in deference to the sensitive nature of his inquiries. We were both aware by the recorded voice on the phone that constantly interrupted our conversation with the message: "All calls are monitored…" We knew that any talk of eliminating people would have to be facilitated through other means.

Once Frankie and I had reached a roadblock in our talks, he stepped aside and allowed L to return to her seat in the glassed booth. She was clearing new tears from her now flushed cheeks.

In her attempt to present a supportive face, she delivered back-to-back one-liner jokes. Normally, I would find anything she said to be amusing, but at this moment I could only contemplate the question that Frankie posed. Thankfully, the visit was coming to an end. L placed her hands on the glass, which fit into the outline of my opened hand. That was the extent of the interaction we could share. Without any further protest, we ended the visit.

If I stayed in this place much longer, I would surely lose her. She was innocent at times, but she was young and she had desires that required daily attention. She had been raised in a structured home, which forced her to remain chaste through her high school years, and even in her early adult life, she had never found anyone to release her sexually—at least that was the tale that she told me. I knew that there wasn't a way she would maintain a sexless existence for much longer. The only logical thing for me to do would be to release her from my heart in order to save my sanity.

As I walked the halls, an officer observed that I looked like I hadn't eaten much. As it stood, I was now a shell of my former self. My fragile health was evident: pale face, prominent cheekbones, and my once lively eyes had receded, giving me the appearance of a starved hostage. My persistent cough was a part of my conversation with L, and it refused to leave.

Even in my lowest moment, I noticed the legion of shapely women who filed out of the visit area. Some seemed to be prancing like newly minted peacocks, with their round hips testing the stitching on their tight jeans. Some even maintained their sex appeal while cradling screaming children on their hips. Interestingly, I noticed how several of the Latin women resembled the characters that filled the tattooed bodies of the gangsters. True to the characters that were displayed on the bodies were the women that wore one too many layers of makeup that accented their look. They appeared to take pride in achieving the proper arch to their intricately drawn-on eyebrows—three Cholas; one newborn child; five prepubescent girls wearing clothes that a discerning mother would protest. The weekly pilgrimage for these ladies seemed like a part of life, almost easy, like it was a part of the deal when engaged to a criminal. All of their proclamations of love appeared natural. L would never submit to this lifestyle.

Once back in the discomfort of dorm life, I decided that I would spend as much time as possible in a hermetic space of silence. I didn't have the energy to be amongst a group of any kind. My reserved posture would mislead several people into thinking that I was asleep, which allowed me to monitor the exchange of war stories. One of the new arrivals to the dorm was most entertaining as he began with several outlandish stories of his bravery. I doubted whether anyone believed his tales, but as he launched into one after the other, it was clear that he hoped his status would be raised. He desperately wanted people to believe that he was skilled in all forms of combat. I laughed to myself, as I wondered how the story would evolve with the passage of time: Would he shuffle the bodies and adjust the level of his participation? Absent the opponent, the voracity of the storyteller remains unknown. I knew that the persona he had embraced would eventually be challenged in this world, and all would see if he were in fact who he claimed to be.

I had grown tired of the war stories and called up memories of L, which only caused me to become filled with jealousy. I felt a sense of proprietorship over her body. I was aware that at the visit, she saved my ego and reassured me that she would remain mine, but in reality, her words meant little. I had become consumed with the mental image of her fulfilling her desires with someone else. I was now torturing myself as I questioned her smile. I knew it was meant to comfort me, but now I wonder if it was a clue that she knew I was aware that she was perpetrating a fraud against our love? I had already learned that she was a skilled fibber, and had she pursued acting as a profession, without a doubt, she would have been world class. But I had caused this hell that I was stuck in. It wasn't fair for me to place restrictions on L. If I were going to have a future—aside from just having L—I would have to win this trial.

I was preparing to walk to the restroom when I noticed two Crips reaching the end of civility as they resorted to the only option that remained in their playbook: hand-to-hand combat. The clash was, sadly, more like a pathetic catfight. But I had to watch. It was a fight; it was entertainment. Their squared stances reflected their lack of fight knowledge and they seemed more concerned with style rather than the effectiveness of their blows. They didn't look to have confidence in their performances, and they knew they just had to exchange knuckles long enough to prove that they were willing—five wildly arraigned punches followed by three sad punches of the same value. The contest would come to an end as the lookout alerted them to an approaching officer. "Pathetic" is what I said as I passed. I was hoping that one of them heard me, so I could put on a boxing clinic for all those that fancied themselves tough. I wanted to show that I was alive, and an exhibition of violence would most certainly get this crowd moving.

I hoped that I would finally be able to establish a lifeline when I placed a call to L. The robotic voice recording served as a warning that our conversations were monitored. I wondered if it were possible for the authorities to monitor all the calls that were placed. It was an interesting study in sycophancy to think that in some dark room sat a technician that was charged with reviewing my life, which had become reduced to sound bites and cryptic messages. Someone would have to invent the worlds that I talked about. I knew that L wouldn't mind someone listening in on the details of how we lived out fantasies in the bedroom, as if she were comfortable with exhibitionism.

Immediately upon answering, L steered the conversation to playful chats about sex. L knew that she wouldn't be able to suppress her sexual thoughts, so in the chat, she made it clear to me that she was naked and preparing herself for a bath, where she would fuck herself slowly. Each time I tried to change the talk to the reality I was facing, but L swiftly steered the talk to her burning desire to be fucked.

I had spent my days since my arrest in complete control of my desires, but once I saw L, those desires awoke with force. I now have to battle nature in a society that holds what is natural in contempt. All remedies that one could use for relief have effectively become criminalized. In addition to my legal battles and these violent officers and gangsters that I am anchored to, I will now have to delay sex. Acts that are natural and healthy—and to some, a ritual—can land you in solitary confinement with an additional criminal charge if one pursues the act while in prison. All L wanted to do was talk about our pleasurable moments. This would prove to be a challenge.

L continued with her sex talk. She panted and said she was touching herself. She knew that I couldn't do much to help her, besides listen and occasionally answer yes to her questions of whether I wanted her to continue, so I listened and answered yes whenever she needed me to give her permission to do what she was already in the process of doing.

In the days that followed I was able to carry on with a schedule. I was careful to watch my conversations with my fellow penitents. I followed the orders of the sheriffs, by being prepared for counts and being ready when asked to recite my booking number: 8511329. I would rise every day and scan the obituaries, hoping to come across the name of my accuser. I had become consumed with the possibility of his death bringing about life for me. I paid little attention to the vigilant guards for both sides. Out of boredom I had allowed myself to participate in the group prayer. It was entertaining to me how the preacher engaged the dorm in a creative way. He began each group with, "Our father, who art in heaven. Hallowed be thy name," and immediately, he would pause at the question, "Whose father?" and the group would respond with, "Our father!" This to me was theater. This was my life for now.

New inmates would arrive and Biggie would administer his obligatory introduction into our world. Biggie's opposite for the SS carried out his intro in the same fashion—granted, the SS penalty for an inmate-imposed rule violation was akin to a death sentence, which may be the reason that the new inmates that align with the SS listen much more closely.

This was my theater: watching new inmates enter the unit with their tough-guy personas glued to their faces, but wondering, as I did, what would happen if they said no? How much time would they have before the group assembled an attack team?

I had gathered the strength to call my mother. As I imagined she would, she greeted me with her love and support. I told her that I couldn't be on the call for too long, as I wanted to call my grandfather. The truth was that I couldn't bear the sound of her voice as she reassured me that everything was going to be okay. I had placed her through hell with my criminal endeavors, and in the pursuit of wealth I had grown apart from my family.

At the end of the call, I dialed Walter's number. The mechanical operator advised him that the call was being monitored and what the price of the collect call would be and that "to accept, press one; to reject, press two."

I expected that he would press two. But then, surprisingly, I heard him say, "Hello."

"Granddaddy, how are you?" I didn't have much to say. Walter was the one person that I had wanted to impress in life, the man that I looked to emulate in style, speech, and ambition. Whenever I succeeded in school or made waves in business, I called to share my good fortune to thank him—often he took credit for my success, even when he rejectedhelping me at the infancy of the venture. Conversely, whenever I walked my way into a bind, Walter left me to figure it out. Unlike with my mother, who I believe gave me room to figure out life and in turn never put the pressure on me to be present for family gatherings, I often wondered if Walter cared if I came or not.

Whatever my suspicions of how my mother and Walter responded to my life choices, I was now faced with a situation that

I could not avoid even if I wanted to; the mechanical operator advised us of my predicament with the often repeated message: "This call is from a correctional facility and is subject to monitoring." With that announcement, I tried my hand at levity, "Well, now that we got that understood, what's new with you?" Walter allowed himself to laugh before he turned on that voice that had command. There wasn't a way that I could see where we would recover a relationship—I knew that I had lost him forever.

Each day the sun came through the mesh screen covering the windows. I began rising before the sun to go through a stretch routine, to combat the effects of lying on paper-thin cots. I had come into possession of a secret that other people in the dorm were not privy to. No one knew that they were going to witness a suicide. My only dilemma was when would I do it? In my dreams I plotted the crime, taking into account every detail. Pharmaceuticals would be my weapon of choice.

There was too much free time on my hands that allowed me to worry about the hacking cough that haunted me. I had reasoned that this sickness was not so much in my body, as it had consumed my soul. The only benefit of the cough was that I had an excuse for not wanting to engage in trivial conversation with the characters that surrounded me. That was the only benefit I could have with these consumptive lungs: it would be used to help me avoid characters that I didn't want in my space.

I had a court appearance and so I was awake even earlier than usual. For those that sought the guidance of the gods, the prayer group was made available in the front of the dorm. I sat at a safe distance and viewed the performance of the preacher in silence.

Many in the group believed that the pious penitents that frequented the prayer group would be delivered from their trials. I only saw the believers return from court expressing hatred for their god. On occasion some would come to express how they now believed that their god was nothing more than a capricious sadist. Most in the group expected deliverance, and they blindly followed the preacher as he encouraged them to "ask, and you shall receive." Rarely did I hear the group question what had brought them to their knees.

There wouldn't be a trial today, only the filling of motions and updates from both sides. This dance of death would continue every thirty days that we agreed to extend. With each appearance in court, I looked on at the friends that sat in the audience and they looked on with lowered gazes, like mourners at a funeral. Several of my friends seemed betrayed as details of my life that they had been oblivious to were revealed. The district attorney seemed to take perverse pride in exposing salacious details of the case, which he had yet to prove true. He knew that, as of now, he didn't have to prove; he just had to allege and isolate me. This was his show, and I was made to watch and agree to the delay.

In the times that I appeared in court, I would notice how the district attorney rules the courtroom. My attorney advised me not to put much thought into the antics of the district attorney, since as it stands, he is not bound by the rules of slander—whatever is revealed while in court, no matter if it's inadmissible, they have immunity. The fight is one where the accused has his hands tied behind his back. The district attorney and the judges are employees of the government. If I didn't have Ron present to drive a wedge, it is more than likely that I would've been steamrolled.

I returned from court to the same humiliating body exam, disgusted that I had mastered the process—three coughs while bent at the waist with my insides exposed was satisfactory for the sadist that viewed me. I had given in to the routine, and in doing so, the sheriffs could only allow me to continue on to the next stage of the gauntlet. My persistent cough had replaced the last prerogative of my natural inclination to challenge injustice. I had submitted. I was now fully engaged to the other side of the coin for a criminal: incarceration.

Rock and Roll

"This morning I watched the destruction of the world as an attentive spectator, then I got back to work…"—Kafka

FRANKIE DEPOSITED MONEY INTO my jail account, allowing me to purchase hygiene and other items from the commissary, which sold ten-cent containers of Top Ramen for ninety cents alongside a host of salt and pepper and ketchup and other packets all marked "not for individual resale." There was no way to survive off of the food provided, and one could bankrupt your supporters just by ordering the basic rations.

There was also a black market. If you were willing to spend ten bucks for a one-dollar hamburger, you could have it delivered to you by the night count. The rumor that a female officer was available for rent was finally confirmed, when I overheard the last part of the negotiations that were underway in the hallway, "two hundred to jack him off and five hundred for head." Those were the terms that Biggie conveyed to a potential client. I saw the sometimes sex-worker officer, and I wouldn't have done it even if she were the one paying me.

Everyone paced the floor, anxiously awaiting the commissary. The SS were forced to provide charity to a "kitty." One by one they would make deposits into a bag, as if they were making sacrifices to the gods. The kitty was used for new arrivals that didn't have hygiene. A new SS could take from the kitty, but once he shopped, he would have to restock the kitty with 10 percent of what he was going to spend at the store. And even a casual observer could see that this taxation caused several SS to talk in private circles about walking away from their shaky alliance.

On the other side of the isle, the Brothers' charitable contributions were voluntary. There were far too many alpha-male personalities in the group to submit to oppressive rules like the ones the SS placed on their followers. I would repay Biggie for the contributions he made to my well-being when I first entered the dorm. He enjoyed pastries, and so I put together a package of sugary products and placed them in his hands without much hype to what I had done.

The night's festivities on the day that the commissary was delivered showed me how humans have the ability to improvise. I started to understand how the ghoulish ritual of the last meal for the condemned had a place in our society. There was comfort in food; it provided sustenance and it was proving that it could calm a rowdy group. This group carried on with odd rituals as they prepared their celebratory meals. Without much hassle, inmates converted the middle bunk into a table. Goods were exchanged like this was the floor of the stock market. I had to acknowledge that I was in the midst of a functioning society. I sat and watched the dorm buzz with activity, and I was certain that this was a society that I didn't want to remain in any longer.

I sought refuge on my perch with a pastry and a cup of hot tea. The pastry had its flaws, but it was all that was available, so without delaying the event I sawed into my glazed bun and reflected on the trite saying that Biggie often invoked: "It could be worse."

The festivities came to a close as the night officers arrived to conduct their count. Like every night before, the preacher gathered his flock and held a group prayer. The preacher never allowed the divisive politics of jail to dictate his commitment of providing guidance to anyone who was seeking the spiritual component to help explain their physical journey. In the last days, he had become humbled in his rhetoric. On this night, there wouldn't be any bombastic speeches or laying of the hands that is present in the Baptist tradition. The preacher instead spoke with a calm that conveyed a savant-like sympathy for his flock. I wondered what in his life had changed.

It was past 1:00 a.m. and I was chasing sleep. I was a perpetual victim to my cough and the cruel thought that I was free. I was resigned to the sad reality that I was not going to be able to enjoy the only act that allowed me pleasure—sleep. The only benefit of not being able to sleep was that I would finally see the night activities that, until now, I had little interest in viewing.

Kaos had warned me about a brute and his crew of flunkies. As it is with most crews in this place, they weren't bona fide tough guys but merely a sad group of adolescent punks from some Compton Crip gang. Their power rested in the group as they walked the dorm, terrorizing weaker inmates. They often channeled their attention onto the female night officer who sat at the desk, on the other side of a grilled gate, believing that they could persuade the officer that they only could enhance her life if she would do their bidding and smuggle in contraband. They had yet to achieve that mission.

Prior to my arrival, Kaos said that he witnessed the crew abduct a rival off his bunk as he slept. The victim left the building shortly after, naked and bleeding from his backside. They proved to Kaos that they were bloodthirsty war criminals who craved excitement.

I watched as the lone brute walked the dorm without his crew. He had the appearance of an old man suffering arthritis pain in his joints, or maybe the bumbling walk was the result of the burden of his life. I figured it best that I keep the brute in sight. He and his flunkies had violent rituals that made it appear that blood was a necessary ingredient in their diet.

I had to relieve myself, which meant I would have to pass the lone brute. I was firm in my decision to attack him first if he came within my zone. I reasoned that it would be better for my existence to err on the side of caution rather than allow him the advantage of having the first blow. He continued with his labored walk, and I continued to watch his movements.

I returned to my bunk and pulled out of my traveling satchel a card from the mail that I had begun to stockpile. I had several pieces of mail from my friend M. In her cards there was no talk of my predicament. She worked at taking my mind out of the world that I was trapped in by allowing me into hers. Her work and family life entertained me greatly. She often sent cards and photographs of her animals and wrote notes in the voice of her dogs. I imagined that when she wrote these words, she was curled up on her couch on a lazy day. She was attempting to relieve my pain, but only freedom would truly bring me calm.

The days would dribble on in the same fashion: Inmates would be transferred in and out of the dorm for court. Inmates would become victims to the system that they pledged allegiance to. I studied the obituary names. Inmates participated in prayer, only to wake up and see that their prayers were in the queue. And my irritating cough remained.

I stood in line to receive the prescription of two Tylenol and to drink lots of water, coincidentally the same prescription had been given to the inmate ahead of me in line for his infected toenail. Another inmate that had a rash covering his side was also given the same prescription of Tylenol and water. I added my health to my list of things that I prayed for.

Days after witnessing the neutered version of the violent brute, it was alarming to see him confined to his bunk foregoing his nightly stalking of the dorm. This was a welcome relief. Maybe his violent streak had come to an end, or so I had hoped. Right as I allowed myself to drift off into the dream world, not expecting that I would be deposited back into the violent real world I lived in, there was a cry for help.

"Man down," rang out—the distress call that inmates and guards reserved for someone who was having a medical emergency.

I woke up fast, wiping clouds from my eyes. The lead brute was hanging from a sheet he had fixed to the grill gate at the far end of the bathroom. Biggie pulled the noose from his neck, while two inmates held his body to relieve the weight. Even from the distance of my bunk I could see that a pasty blue flesh tone had covered his face. His soiled pants were an indicator that he was far into his escape plan.

The officers made their way to the dorm, barking orders from the safe side of the gate, "Get down! Everybody get to your fucking bunks!" The officers nervously waited for the assembled inmates to clear the area before they entered. The officers would scream their orders again as they waited for Biggie and two other inmates that had stayed with the brute, assisting him with breathing.

Biggie worked his breathing maneuvers on the brute until he had restored the natural brown color to the brute's face. He then relieved himself of his post, allowing the nervous officers to enter with the medical staff—five officers entered; seven assembled on guard at the gate. The brute was carted out of the dorm with little care, as the gurney slammed against the walls and gate with force. I could see a vacant look fixed to the brute's eyes as the gurney passed. He looked to be a man who fully realized that he was a failure. He couldn't even control his own act of suicide.

Shortly after the officers cleared the dorm of any criminal wrongdoing, the preacher stood at the head of the dorm and acted out a eulogy for the brute. I then realized that the dorm had unknowingly allowed the preacher's constant vigil to set the stage for how the dorm would end each night. He was humbled in his daily prayers, as it served as the basis for how he displayed his faith. But, on this occasion, for the first time, the entire dorm was at attention and ready to join in prayer. The preacher had what he had desired all along: complete obedience to him.

The skeptic in me wondered if the preacher had orchestrated the suicide. I had seen the preacher and the brute conversing on occasion, and I can see the situation where the preacher may have given him his blessing to walk to the other side. I held this theory, but I would never share it with anyone else. I would just watch as the preacher's flock grew. One by one they stood, pledging allegiance to the church of the preacher. I refused to follow the converted; Kaos saw me eyeing the crowd and in an attempt to lighten the mood asked when I would be saved.

"If there is going to be any spiritual awakening, it will take place on my terms and at my bed." And without hesitation, I retired. There wasn't anything I could do to help the brute.

The weekend had come and L rewarded me with a visit. I worked hard to put on a strong face, hoping that she wouldn't notice how weak I had become. No man is a hero to his butler, and I knew that I wouldn't be able to fool L. She had guided me back to health before, and she knew the difference between me in discomfort and me in pain. I couldn't complete a sentence without the grubby cough interrupting. I could only hope that I wouldn't scare her away before the visit had ended.

I didn't allow myself to celebrate with L's Saturday visit—it had seemed to be more of a charitable act on her part than something she actually enjoyed. She'd vacillated between laughter and heart-stopping sadness, managed to lower her reply to my "I love you" down to one second. Every topic was cut short by the elephant in the room: my upcoming trial. She shed her usual amount of tears. The duration of the flow was all a part of L's performance.

Between the phone calls and the occasional visit, we had run through all of our stories, and we decided to resort to the trick of creating fictitious sexual experiences of what we will do once I am free. L merged actual experiences with the invented ones, and in each scenario she was careful to remind me how pleasing I was as a lover. The fantasy of fiction was the only escape for the hour-long visit. But it was fiction. The water-filled eyes that looked at me through the glass would most certainly be fixed on another lover soon.

The officer gave the visitors the five-minute hand gesture. We placed our palms on the window, and I watched as L's hand fell in the shadow of mine. I saw hints of the innocent girl that I had fallen for. She was still a girl who had plenty of life to experience. It would be selfish for me to demand her time for much longer.

L fled for the exit as she professed her love for me. She seemed more eager to leave this place than other times. I couldn't fault her for holding contempt for this process. She didn't sign up for this life. My transgression had thrust this dirt onto her and I wondered how long she would mourn our love once she decided to end it for good.

The days would stumble on. But one day I was left to wonder what was causing the alarm in the dorm. There wasn't an event that I could pinpoint that adjusted the atmosphere, but without much talk, soldiers on both sides took up positions and awaited the approval to clash. It was clear that conflict was on the horizon, and I would now get the opportunity to act out violently, and sadly set the stage for how I would be viewed moving forward by my peers.

Within five seconds of soldiers migrating to safety zones, we heard the dorm above explode with the rumbling of feet. The slamming of metal bunks and shuffling of feet sounded like a symphony being conducted in hell. The groups in our dorm paused, waiting for a sign that other dorms were participating—an indicator that it was a coordinated attack by a group. The shocked faces and lack of movement by the SS indicated that it wasn't.

The officers ran to the alarm, leaving our dorm unsupervised. The heads of the groups took that opportunity to discuss the war that had erupted above us, and how our dorm would respond. Because my position in the defensive formation had me posted in the rear flank, I was not in range to hear where the talks were going and if war would visit our dorm. As the tear gas bombs exploded, my hearing became mute, which caused me to rely solely on the movements of my fellow fighters over any orders that might've been delivered from Biggie. We stood looking up to the ceiling, listening to feet as they traced the battlefield. The scratching of metal on the concrete provided the image of where the bunks were headed.

The separation of the dorms was likening to being in completely different parts of the same city. The only mixing was when we shared the recreation yard, or the brief interaction walking to and from visiting. The heads were given the "keys" to a dorm or a yard and were charged with being the representative and the chief executive for the organization. The dorm I was assigned to has maintained the peace through diplomacy, and now, along with everyone else, I looked on as the heads talked, wondering how strong the accord was.

The battlefield of survivors cautiously filed into our dorm with the stench of pepper spray and sweaty blood still present on their bodies. Joe and Biggie continued their talks with the SS, neither side allowing their confident posture to be betrayed. The officers that stood on the other side of the gate laughed as they waited for our dorm to erupt in war.

I stood ready for battle, knowing that at any moment, blood would be spilled—hoping that it would not be mine—and without disappointment, Biggie made the first move when he raised his knife, bringing it down onto the face of the SS leader, slicing a clean line that stretched from the forehead to his chin in the process, a brilliant crimson river replacing the sweat on the SS's face. He'd used a simple tool, adapted for use in his environment. Eleven, possibly thirteen inches was the length of the opening.

The sad little man that served as the executive officer for the SS leader stood, frozen as a totem pole as his comrade became a victim to the knife. Their organization had given much thought to royal rituals and performances, as they realized that their kingship was created entirely by the way their subjects reacted to them, and they feared an event like this one.

The Brothers followed Biggie's bold move with quick decisive blows to any SS in striking range, and in the process eliminating the advantage the SS once had with their numbers. Without a pause, the soldiers charged ahead, pulling knives from hidden compartments, taking aim at their targets.

Kaos and I had discussed what we would do if we were presented with this scenario. I noticed that he took up a position on the opposite end of the dorm. The cluster of SSs he was with seemed content with holding position against a wall. I was relieved that Kaos and I wouldn't face one another. But, without hesitation, I reacted by unleashing a flurry of shots at the first SS that moved in my direction.

Every brother seemed possessed with the strength of five men; even the scout DTG who usually removed himself from the drama of the dorm was seen snapping punches at another opponent. He made it clear that he was as comfortable waging war as he was with living in peace.

There were less than twenty-nine Brothers in the dorm doing battle with over eighty SS. It was an unavoidable thought that the sheriffs had assigned more SS to the dorm to watch how they would try to establish dominance, which ultimately would cause conflict. It was unlikely that the authorities failed to consider how one side would take advantage of having more soldiers than the other. Putting aside the motives of the officers, both sides knew that they had to fight.

The officers positioned themselves on the other side of the gate in full riot gear. With precise moves, they opened the square slots in the gate and began to fire shots from the various weapons in their arsenal. Any moving body was a target to the shooters at the gate. The sound of pellets zipping across my head served as the alarm that the war would soon come to an end, but, until it did, I had to continue to fight. The opponent who was advancing in my direction stopped as several pellets hit him, causing him to retreat. The retreat allowed me to turn my attention to helping a Korean associate of mine that was defending himself from the advances of two SS. The SS would also retreat as they were hit by pellet shots, and in that moment, we turned our attention from the SS to the officers that continued to fire shots—and then the thundering sound of bombs going off filled the dorm.

There were several booms of concussion grenades being released onto the dorm, causing a blanket of thick smog to loom. The pellet shots continued inches from my head. I was surprised and relieved that I hadn't been hit. The officers' commands for everyone to get down were the permission that everyone was waiting for to give up the fight. The battle for me ended in the bathroom, as I lay flat in the prone position, barely inches from the urine trough.

Moving in tactical formation, the officers covered the dorm with their pellet guns trained on the crowd. Both sides that had waged war against each other were now captives to the officers. They had nonlethal weapons and the authority to use them to maintain the safety and security of the institution. Most wouldn't admit that they were relieved that the officers had put an end to the event, but the victims of Biggie's wrath would not deny the help that the officers provided.

The partitioning of the dorm hadn't provided security as the political leaders had intended. The reasoning for segregation and the war remained a mystery to me. Some of the participants came alive when the war began, as if they welcomed a break from the monotony of our bleak existence. Some of the veterans wore extra shirts to cover their mouths from airborne irritants as preparation for what happens at the end of a war, evidence of their own familiarity with how these events normally played out: with every inmate gasping as they inhaled copious amounts of chemicals.

Time passed and parts of my vision came back and I was able to make out an SS being wheeled out of the dorm, holding a bleeding wound to his abdomen. I was lying inches from a piss trough, yet I found the time to admire how exotic the female officers appeared when in their full riot regalia. They tried hard to assert their authority, but it all read as a joke, as the women imitated the male officers' cocked-legged stances, unaware that instead of displaying their maleness, they unknowingly put on display the V shape that formed in between their legs.

The chemical fog may have been what I needed to clear my lungs, because once I started to cough, a bolus of phlegm was ejected from my lungs. I was free of my cough.

The officers moved as if stepping through a minefield. The fog of irritants didn't faze them as they breathed with the assistance of state-of-the-art masks. They too were veterans of prison combat. The group leader barked orders for the rank and file to "bag and tag" the dorm. The process of cleaning up in the aftermath was conducted with care for the officers' safety; an inmate bleeding was left to suffer with his wound until the officer considered it appropriate to remove him from the battlefield. Two officers would supervise a four-man chain of inmates as the dorm moved in a line to the recreation yard. The officers once again had a captive audience.

The fog of the dorm was replaced with the cold night air. For the first time since my incarceration, I took in the night sky. The fresh air was a welcome gift for the victors and the defeated, as we stood shoulder to shoulder to submit to a body scan.

The night air and the nerve-twisting events caused the testicles of some to retreat inward for warmth, and as the process continued, I was relieved at having little room for prudish modesty or embarrassment. There I stood, naked as a newborn, confident that I would make a proper impression if one of the female officers looked at my torso area during inspection. "Cough, spread your ass, lift up your nuts, re-grip!" were usually orders the male officers barked in body scans, but because of the event, I had the privilege of performing our sadistic ritual for a woman.

I had survived my first "rock and roll," as Biggie called it. But after having participated in the event, it was clear that what I had originally thought was true; the politicians believed that going to war would serve the failed political talks of the dorm, but as we sat—captives to a common foe—it was obvious that this war only served to enrich our captives as they logged in their overtime pay.

In society, if a bullet doesn't kill you or render you an indolent, the wound becomes a badge of honor, a conversation starter. But, in this world, where creative inmates have been known to marinate knives in feces with the intention of passing on to the victim some horrible infection along with an unsightly flesh wound, you quickly realize that a prison wound can carry with it more history than a simple bullet wound. In this hole, one maintains hyper-alert to avoid war wounds; the rolled, hunched shoulders, the defensive stances, and the separating of the sides to avoid interaction all served a purpose. This was my new life.

The perimeter lights lit the yard, setting the atmosphere of a sports arena. I had taken my thoughts far from the yard where I was, and was able to see in the distance, the blinking lights of a plane. I imagined that it was carrying ordinary people to an exotic location. I allowed my thoughts to roam while sitting handcuffed, naked. I now wondered how much endurance I really possessed. I thought about the defeated, and how or when they would want their revenge.

My thoughts went to the brute that attempted suicide. How did Biggie know that he wanted to be saved? He went to great lengths to braid the sheets so that it could support his weight. He was well prepared to die. I wondered how he was adjusting to the padded cell in the psychiatric ward—he would've enjoyed this war.

I noticed the preacher looking on with the sad broken eyes of a basset hound. I wanted to laugh at him, just so he could see that his attempts to unify us savages under the name of Christ was a futile endeavor. We were the animals that the officers said we were, and we belonged exactly where we were: caged.

It was clear that the SS had sustained a loss. If there was a victory, it wasn't because of the physical triumph by the Brothers—

it had more to do with the SS premise being predicated on a faulty assumption that they could actually reclaim California through any means other than at the ballot box. But here they sat, victims of their own stupidity.

Zip Codes

After the War

"Events that move the world enter on doves' feet." —Nietzsche

I WALKED WITH A group of eleven battle-tested inmates down the same musty hallway that I had been walking since I arrived in Wayside. But, because of my performance in the melee, I now walked the hallways with a target on my back. Before Biggie and I parted ways, he warned me to be aware of how the SS monitored my movements going forward. The group I walked with would be ushered into our new dorm wearing only boxer shorts to cover our bodies. We were the examples of how creatively inhumane the authorities can be in the administration of justice. This was proof to anyone looking on that no matter the side you're on, war is hell.

The inhabitants of the dorm we entered studied our every move. They suspected that we would infect their world with the ills that caused ours to implode. Most were in deep thought, studying card and chess games without the loud back-alley casino talk that was ever present in most dorms that I had been assigned to. The eyes of the players examined us as we waited to have the obligatory conversations with the representatives. And on cue, we were approached.

A young guy approached the group of Brothers that I entered the dorm with, advising us that he spoke for the Brothers. He would launch into his speech with much pride as he advised us that he was known by the name Mad Bone, from Inglewood Bloods. I imagined that he was a menace with a weapon while in society, because his physical appearance didn't look like what you would expect to see when you heard the name Mad Bone. He was rail thin with feet like duck flappers and a face that appeared stretched to comedic proportions as he delivered the house rules. Before Mad Bone finished his talk, he leaned in and added at the end, "We know what went down."

It was clear that the elders in this dorm enjoyed their table games. Having the ability to participate in card games presented an opportunity to challenge workable complexities and obtain a level of mastery over a game in an environment completely beyond our control. Pinochle, Black Jack, Bridge, and Spades were preferred over Texas Hold'em Poker, as one old-timer remarked in what I would come to know as his trash talk, "This ain't for no bitches… bring your ass to the table, and be prepared to stay all night." I was relieved to be amongst thinkers on both sides of the isle.

The SS here were noticeably older than the inmates I had just battled against. The same rules applied—partitioning of the dorm tables and phones was standard for every dorm. The difference, however, was in their attitudes. They didn't seem to be in a proving state of their life. Their faces told the tales.

I wasn't surprised to see that I would be in a middle coffin, just like the last one. I figured it best to proceed cautiously, considering that I was fresh from the battlefield. I made it a point to exchange pleasantries with my neighbors that sat around in small talk. I knew that they all were aware that I was one of the participants in a war that may have sent some of their comrades to the infirmary, and I didn't know how they would see their role in the event.

After several failed attempts, I made contact with L. I didn't dare share what I had just experienced with the war and the restructuring of the dorms. She was a civilian, and she would apply civilian logic to a world where logic is set aside for the rules that the officers and the gangs believe would best serve the population. I knew it best to leave her blind to my world, or risk having to expose her to another part of this world that would only justify her position when she decided to leave me.

The childish excitement in her tone lulled me into believing that she was anticipating my call. Even from the beginning of the call, I had begun to brace myself for the pause in the conversation when I would run out of promising reports. I figured it best when that point began that I would drift into a comfortable silence as she took over the talk with one of her attempts to gain my approval, while she insisted that she was maintaining her fidelity. I understood what was transpiring; her chaste life—only pleasuring herself—was a farce, meant to gain an advantage.

After I ended the call with L, I decided to place one to M, and to my delight, she answered on the first ring. I laughed as she fumbled with her words in response to the mechanical operator who spelled out the procedure of how one was to accept the collect call. I knew that my call to M was a betrayal of my commitment to L, but it was M who was genuinely supporting me in this trial, and L was merely available to exercise my sexual fantasies. I also was certain that L had already set the stage to exit.

My time with M was an extension of our letters. I allowed myself to be candid with her as to my uncertain future. I figured it time that I laid out my list of demands that I had prepared for people that chose to remain supporters, but before I could read from the list, M interrupted and began with what would become understood as the most comforting statement, when she made it known to me that "[She was] not interested in [my] confessions; how can I help?" This was an approach that I could respect. M had an understanding of law and where I stood in the legal system, which meant that I could ask of her things that L and Frankie were unable to comprehend. I knew her presence in my life would anger L, but my options were limited and if there was a verdict of guilty, then there would be no more chances; my fight to survive would be over.

Before we ended our call, M would confess that she had recaptured our past with a voice message that I had left for her when I last phoned. She didn't offer any suggestions on what I should do with this information. I hoped her support stemmed from concern for my life and not with the hope that I would cave into her generosity and desire for love. I knew the answer, and I knew that what I was embarking on with M would end horribly.

I was ushered in and out of another court appearance in less than five minutes. This court appearance was another legal formality, in order to maintain compliance with the judicial clock that dictates criminal procedure. I saw Frankie and M in the crowd, but no L. I had prepared myself for the day when she made her exit. I had hoped she would last longer.

The holding cell often provided me with a moment to myself. I wasn't alone there, but the other inmates were usually lost in thought and no one saw the need for small talk. I thought about how many nights out with L had turned into early mornings at cafes, our sunglasses suddenly useful again. Sometimes we'd go from the nightclub to the ocean and sit watching the tides roll in and out. L's company was comforting, and she'd confessed the same to me on many mornings.

I wondered how long the memory would remain for L.

The bus climbed onto the 110 Freeway at a snail pace for 109 seconds. I shared the space with forty-three inmates and when I added myself and the officers that guarded us, I laughed at the number forty-seven, as it was a prime number. I hoped that my tallying of people and objects wouldn't over take my thoughts where I would eschew my vigilant observance for safety.

While on the bus rides from court, I had begun a custom of silently praying for the occupants of the cars behind us as chunks of death blanketed the road every time the driver pushed the accelerator. These chunks of pollution that billowed out were entertainment as we waited to see how unsuspecting drivers reacted to the black smoke being expelled. One unsuspecting driver would adjust his head to protest, only to retreat back into his car as he realized that he would be barking at the LA County Sheriff's transportation bus, not knowing who was being held inside. As usual, the bus churned on, bullying smaller vehicles.

The weekend approached, and as expected, L didn't find it necessary to visit, nor was it a priority of hers to provide me the courtesy of relaying a message that she was alive. She chose not to answer my calls for days, which further frustrated me, as I had few options of making contact with her. I was engaged in a one-way relationship. She controlled every moment.

M didn't permit me much free time to wallow in misery. Letters from her were answering questions I had asked, and she decided to make the sacrifice of waiting hours in line to visit whenever I asked. M was careful in her assessment of my risk-taking. I knew that she wanted to, but she never admonished me for my criminal decisions. She regarded our visits and phone conversations to be a time of discovery and not a space for incriminations. I chose to believe that M and Frankie both looked past the baggy jumpsuit and the gaunt face to the man that they knew still existed.

Initially I found it disturbing that my neighbor was able to sleep around the clock. His comrades woke him up for security counts— food was an occasional luxury that he allowed himself—but it was clear that he didn't want to wander too far from his bunk. He proved to be creative as I noticed how he converted toothpaste into tape and hung pictures of his children, interspersed with pornographic-style photos of bikini-clad women, and in the moments that he chose to grace the dorm with his attention, he performed a routine that bordered on obsessive as he kissed and held conversations with the pornographic women and his children with ease, only to return to his dream world.

He and other inmates had become pleasure-seekers who embraced sleep as if it were the equal to sex. I couldn't understand how they were able to unplug from life for the hours that they did; then I saw the affair they had with sleep was facilitated by pills. This dorm was comprised of a herd of pharmacological animals that roamed in a dream state. Their limited conversations were proof that they had become connoisseurs of the many downers. They perfected the keywords that the therapist needed to obtain the desired pills and dosage necessary to help them into the dream world. This was a creative, albeit drugged group.

I didn't have the desire to indulge in drugs for a bedtime elixir, but I did recognize that I could begin to stockpile pills in the event I decided to end my ordeal, if my trial was a failure. With enough pills, I could drift in my normal biorhythmic transition and simply slip away. The possibility that this was going to end for me with the sentence of life in prison was not a scenario that I was going to wait to come to pass. I believed that I had devised the perfect crime that I could never be prosecuted for.

I had grown comfortable with my future crime and how I would carry it out. I had begun to store my pills in my satchel that I kept lodged in between my buttocks. I didn't worry about the officers in the hallways, as most had become accustomed to my presence on the compound and rarely was I molested in line movements to the yard or visiting. The stage was set, but I hoped I wouldn't have to go on with this role.

We Will be Loved

"For a country is considered the more civilized the more the wisdom and efficiency of its laws hinder a weak man from becoming too weak or a powerful one too powerful."
—Primo Levi

SHE SAT ACROSS FROM me with a devilish grin fixed on her face. Her presence consumed all the space in my mind, and for a second my faith in the commitment we once shared had been restored. I believed her presence meant that there was hope for our relationship, but to save myself the embarrassment, I kept my thoughts to myself. It had taken L five seconds to profess her love for me.

Before I could inquire about her delinquent state, L abruptly excused herself under the pretense that she had to use the restroom. I didn't object and instead enjoyed the view of her backside as she walked away.

Upon returning, she sat and quickly revealed that she was holding her panties. I looked on, unable to speak as she playfully tugged at the soft cotton. She didn't seem concerned with anyone that might see that she was holding her panties, or that she had started to raise her bohemian-style dress to gain access to her hairless pussy. I maintained my silent vigil as she began fingering herself. I didn't dare interrupt and miss any part of her performance.

I was relieved that no one noticed that she was exposed, and as her courage grew she raised her dress, eventually letting it rest at her waist. I was the only witness to this beautiful event; watching as she became lost in sexual transport. L had become completely committed to the act. The only thing I believed I could do was remain silent and enjoy as she reached the next level of pleasure; her eyes closed and her lips parted, and without encouragement from me, she deposited another finger in herself.

One hundred and nine seconds had passed before L's eyes opened as she approached the end of her performance. I couldn't allow myself to blink. This event was meant to stay with me—a gift for the future. She would break the stare as she pulled back her soft hair into an upswept tail. She never spoke a word during our exchange. A nod of approval was all that I could bring myself to do. Her smile conveyed to me that she was comfortable having performed for my pleasure in a public place.

Without much of a rush, L gathered herself and retreated to the restroom. I feared that she wouldn't return, but 181 seconds later, she returned, fully composed and with the often used "I love you" as a greeting. She would refuse to accept my apologies, but I made them known anyways. She tried to hide the reason for her visit, but as the moments dragged on without much to discuss, it was clear that her spirited performance was a parting gift, as this would be the last time that I would see her.

Later that day while in the dorm, I phoned L, but there wasn't an answer. I would place a call to her every thirty-one minutes, thinking that I had missed her as she showered or maybe she couldn't respond to the mechanical secretary in the time allotted as she rushed in the house to answer the phone.

In the dorm environment, the showers turn on for anyone to use every four hours, for thirty-minute runs. Often the water is ice-cold, so I figured out a time when the least amount of people took advantage of the showers, and I could have a few feet of space to myself. On this day I was pleased when I found that not many people were aware that the water was so hot that we had what resembled a proper steam room environment. For once I had an area of the dorm for my pleasure, and in that moment, I became aware of the physical makeups of myself. I was viewing a body that had begun to fail me under the strain of life. I was unrecognizable to myself. Sadly, before I could become completely consumed with my dilemma, I noticed that where I saw the failures in my body, this other person that was now present might have seen an opportunity.

I turned to see how much attention this guy was paying to me or if I had misread what I believed to be interest. I reasoned that his thoughts must've been hijacked by a fantasy that he was intent on playing out, when—with total disregard for what his fate would be if I reported his behavior to his gang—he lowered his gaze. For a second I debated if I should set him straight and let him know that I was not interested in his stares; but I decided against confrontation, as I realized that I was still naked and even a verbal battle would be embarrassing to have while naked.

He may have sensed that I was not going to reciprocate his behavior, so he initiated conversation to lower any animosity that I may have had. Maybe I was being presumptuous in thinking that he was interested in engaging sexually with me. But his constant eyeing of my belt line was leaving me with few options. I tried to reason that glancing was not evidence of a crime in itself, being that anyone who has grown up in a locker room environment will have viewed their share of naked men and even conducted a mental comparison—all in the course of honoring our competitive caveman position—and even with the awkward exchange that was happening, I too compared and was relieved to know that I possessed a superior male organ.

I had known my shower mate, Prieto, from the small talk we shared in the dorm. He was an affable character who pledged allegiance to the SS way of life and even participated in the occasional disciplining of a comrade. I knew that he wasn't the most masculine of gangsters, but I didn't realize that he was so desperate for another human that he would pretend to drop his shower bottle over and over again, each time taking the opportunity to show me his hairless ass.

He was obviously at the mercy of his appetites. If I were to entertain him any longer, I'd be in the midst of an affair. Prieto had created the situation where my solace was being taken for participation and he was going to force me to harm him or report him to his associates, who would most definitely cause him great bodily injury. For his sake, I hoped he didn't act out any further.

I would make it back to my bunk without incident and over the days I'd see Prieto nervously watching me as I engaged in conversation with the SS, not knowing if I was informing on him or if I was merely talking sports. He was in his own self-made hell, where he feared the sound of his name being called.

The SS took the position that homosexuality was deathly prohibited. They would often comment about how the Brothers didn't exterminate a homosexual inmate that was under their care, but I would come to know that the Brothers' attitude toward gay inmates is that they will not be harmed as long as they are not aggressive in their efforts to carry on—which meant no offering of their services.

Over time, Prieto grew comfortable that I would not tell anyone of his effeminate behavior. And with that confidence, I had begun to notice how comfortable he had become with the leader of the SS. It was obvious to the casual observer how the two consistently made trips to the bathroom at the same time. I'd also noticed how they had adjusted their shower time so that they shared space. Their conversations gave one the sense that they were enjoying their courtship. I was hyperaware because I had the unfortunate encounter with Prieto, but I believe others saw the same and knew that the two were in the midst of an affair. For any soldier to question what may be suspected, there would have to be someone willing to risk their life to come forward having ocular proof, considering it was the leader of their crew. It was doubtful that anyone would be prepared to sign an indictment.

I despised walking to the bathroom at night. I would have to strain my eyes to see the clock behind the grilled gate and debate if the officers had already conducted their security check. As it stood, walking the dorm when it was close to security check could draw the unwanted attention of officers that looked forward to confrontation. On this night, I reasoned that I would make my way to the bathroom and be back at my bunk before the check, and if not, then I'd take whatever punishment that would come my way versus further damaging my bladder.

I entered the bathroom in a hurry and there they were, Prieto kneeling before Manny, boldly participating in an affair with the SS leader. The two were tucked in the shower area, lost in their affair, and they never noticed that I had entered the bathroom. In that brief moment that I viewed their interaction, Prieto was taking whatever his leader had to offer with intense and eager enjoyment. I looked long enough to verify that Prieto was a master at fellatio, but not long enough to count strokes to completion as I turned on my heels and exited without disturbing their encounter.

If their actions were ever revealed, Prieto and Manny would be placed on trial and an execution would most certainly follow. Prieto was apparently determined to continue his homosexual behavior under any circumstance—including death.

Over the weeks I would witness Prieto and Manny venturing off to the bathroom at night. During the day, they maintained the mask of the hardened convicts and fully participated in the political system. They were living a double life within the jail system. Visually, Manny looked the part of the prisoner, with his tattooed body and shaved head. But nightly, he made a pilgrimage to the bathroom with Prieto and played another part in a drama that would most definitely end badly if they were to be exposed. This was the height of drama, and I used my knowledge as a vehicle for entertainment.

I had grown accustomed to the activities of the dorm, and I knew not to question why some inmates were carted off on stretchers or why some fled the dorm under the shield of night. I had a view of the dorm from my bunk and every day my voyeuristic itch was satisfied with some form of drama unfolding. I'd also see that the whispers always served as the omen for the violence that would soon follow. And, without fail, I would receive another dose of violent entertainment.

Prieto stood with a gang of SS as they interrogated their newest would-be victim. The victim didn't seem interested in winning the gang over to his position, as he continued with his workout routine in the gap of space at his bunk. The victim stood well over six feet tall and it was apparent with the repetition of his pushups that he was in top physical shape. His face never gave the impression that he was worried or less than confident about his ability to stand up to the growing group of thugs that gathered before him.

Manny made his way from the rear of the dorm, cutting through the crowd of SS with little concern for niceties. I had to consider whether his concern to the group was secondary to his concern for Prieto, his lover, who was leading the confrontation on the victim. I knew that at this point of the affair, there were far too many egos invested in removing this victim, and no one was prepared to walk away, including the victim.

Manny was now standing within inches of the would-be victim, his hands at his side, leaving him defenseless as the "victim" threw an effective right hook that rendered Manny useless. The "victim" immediately turned his offense onto the SSs that were in striking range. His economizing of his punches made it clear that he was trained in combat, versus just someone whom was willing to fight.

The majority of fighting styles the SS used were adequate when it was three of them versus one unskilled victim, but as they faced this pugilist, their flailing style would prove inefficient. And even with the victim holding the momentary upper hand, he knew that it would be impossible to hold off thirty-one wild animals for much longer. So in a move that made clear that he was a pragmatic soldier, he screamed out for the guards.

It was surprising to see the officers respond to the screams so quickly. They closed in on the dorm, spraying chemical agents at attackers and bystanders alike, showing little concern for who was affected. Like every incident before, the wisdom of the officers was to put the entire dorm down, then they could sort out the bodies. Manny lay motionless at the bottom of bodies that the "victim" had piled up. The one perfectly placed punch closed the story on Manny's reign in this dorm.

After the officers cleared the dorm of aggressors and the victim, the story started circulating that the attack was because the victim was being charged with child abuse. In this world, anyone that beats his or her children is likened to a child molester or baby killer. The would-be victim was due to make bail that day, but instead he was forced to do battle. During his brief stay he protested his charges, and apparently went as far as telling the story that his wife had manufactured the charges to gain an advantage in a protracted divorce. That was the only argument he presented to the SS; they didn't want to hear his story.

The various groups usually held a debriefing after a melee to ensure that the other side was clear as to what happened and to issue apologies if their group's issues affected the house. In his first act of diplomacy as the newly minted leader of the SS, Prieto carried out the obligatory talk with the groups. I stood in the rear of the dorm, laughing. Prieto was now left alone to rule as king—or, if he were bold enough to assert his preference, queen.

The Brothers held a junta after Prieto issued apologies on behalf of his group. Trey was the new, democratically elected representative for the group. (Unlike the SS, who are appointed, the Brothers and Others elect their spokesmen.) Trey would prove to be a first-rate intellectual, and from the stories that surrounded his arrival, he also was a war-tested politician keenly aware of the value in diplomacy.

Trey and Manny had agreed that if the failed politics from another dorm made their way to our doorstep, they would not follow the dictates of anyone from the outside. Trey's experience in the ways of his enemy didn't allow him to blindly accept that agreement as gospel; he would let it be known at times that he knew the agreement was nothing more than lip service, as it would be career suicide for an SS to ignore a call to action from the wider leadership. But being the politician that he was, he accepted what Manny had offered.

Trey recognized how demoralized the SS were as the dorm witnessed one man defeat their most energetic soldiers with little more than superficial bruising to indicate that he had been the victim. Trey would adjust his rhetoric as the days passed, opening his arms so that the leadership that he provided would extend to all in the dorm. His talk shifted so that he was now talking in generalities and stressing how the "system" viewed "convicts" and in the process he abandoned the racial superiority bend that other representatives used to rally the troops. He made it clear that he and his brothers would "risk peace every time, without hesitation."

Prieto knew that it would serve his group best if they aligned under one banner of convicts rather than test Trey's position of his group's war readiness. Prieto's crew was ill-equipped and would never match Trey's political genius, and as the days passed, with issue after issue, Prieto would fold his hand and cave in to Trey's position.

Trey spoke the language of the people, but he often adjusted to speak the Queen's English as his audience changed. When speaking with the Spanish-speaking individuals, he spoke in the Castilian dialect. He proved daily to be more than a man merely of words. His use of the Socratic Method when engaging his citizenry in conversation served twofold: He clarified and confused—often drawing laughter from the group. But, above all, he loved hearing himself speak.

A thief in prison is equal to scum from a waste treatment plant. Even if your crime that brought you to jail was theft—robbery, burglary, car—a prison thief was likened to being a baby-killing rapist, or a cop. When people in the dorm started noticing personal items missing from satchels, the dorm enlisted a surveillance squad to monitor the movements of the likely suspects. There weren't many new arrivals, so most people were known to one another, which meant that the thief was someone who knew the chemistry of the dorm, someone who fancied himself sly.

Often the yard is offered on an optional basis. Anytime I had the option I elected to stay in and sleep. Trey assigned two sentinels to keep watch of the dorm and Prieto assigned two of his most trusted meth-addicted soldiers that had already been awake for days to serve as lookouts. My bunk was positioned in the rear of the dorm, close to Prieto, which allowed me to see that his two lookouts had their post at his bunk. I knew what their purpose was and I was confident that I was safe.

The yard returned and so began the normal rush to reserve shower stalls. The dorm was once again filled with movement. Trey and Prieto were having a conversation that was sprinkled with laughter. The miserable excuse of a lunch arrived and the routine of the day continued. And just when all seemed to be routine, Trey's soldiers began making their rounds advising the Brothers that there was a mandatory junta set to take place at the back of the dorm. By this point in my jail stay, I knew that juntas could serve as a way to disseminate information or corral a victim. The blinking eyes that tracked the movements of certain people could almost serve as Morse code danger signals. I was sure that bad things were to follow.

Trey stood with his back to the wall as he addressed the assembled, shared the sad fact that he had fallen victim to thievery. With that revelation, the stale air seemed to be sucked out of the dorm, as everyone waited for clues as to where Trey was going with this story. Before he got to his next sentence, a shifty-eyed character brought attention to himself as he started to ease out of the junta. But unfortunately he found himself cornered and soon fulfilled his role as a punching bag.

Blows rained down on him. The group knew who was marked for death and Trey's contrived speech served as the queue to those assigned to carry out internal enforcement, to act. They showed no mercy to the thief. The three-man hit squad threw forty-one punches and seven kicks between them, with every shot landing at its target.

Once the beating concluded, the mark was allowed to collect his property and exit, alive, albeit broken. Without much fuss, the dorm's movement returned to its normal flow. No one appeared shaken by the violence, and oddly, the mood settled into something resembling jovial. It was as if the violence were as normal as relieving oneself in the bathroom. The attack party didn't break out into any prideful boasting, nor were there any high fives. It all seemed like an ordinary day in Wayside. As the days passed, there weren't any reports of property missing. It's possible that the victim was the thief. There was no doubt that his beating certainly served as a deterrent to anyone else that might want to relieve someone else of their property.

It wouldn't take much for an ordinary man to be impressed in a place where the rule of law is violence first and always. But, here I sat next to Trey on the toilet. Even in this awkward situation, I would come to see Trey's overreaching influence and charm. Two sentinels stood at the entrance. I braced myself for his charm offensive as I realized that conversations that take place while one is relieving oneself are not normal in any environment. The ease with which Trey got the conversation going was proof positive that he was in constant campaign mode, always ready to avail himself to his constituents—wherever he found himself.

He chose his words carefully, pausing for effect, "I wasn't sure if the guy was the thief, but his number had already come up for bitching out in a riot…by taking care of him for that, the SS could rest, believing we took care of the thief. Now, they owe us one. Ma'fuckas will think twice before getting sticky fingers from now on—right?"

He confessed that a beatdown "solved more problems than waiting to catch the real thief...shit, maybe he was." If it weren't clear to me before, Trey would reveal how he viewed some people's lives as bargaining tools. By Trey's assessment, the sacrificial lamb becomes important to the overall peace process that could follow.

I wasn't versed in the proper protocol when engaged in conversations with a politician while on a toilet. I waited for him to wipe before I did. I reasoned that if I followed his lead, then he couldn't gauge my disgust for his political maneuvers. I washed in the sink next to Trey and followed his lead as he exited.

After returning to my bunk, I secured the stockpile of pills to my waistband. Every moment that I wasn't required to be mentally present, I chose to escape to my hermitage and call up the mental images of the world I used to live in. I finished each session with a morbid game of guessing expiration dates. Every three bunks in the row, I'd guess the inmate's age and assign a number of twenty-three for an inmate who appeared to be nineteen, and thirty-seven to an inmate who appeared between the ages of twenty-three and thirty-one. Inmates who looked older than forty-one would be assigned sixty-seven, eighty-three, or eighty-nine. After going through the assignments, I'd cancel out the inmates that looked to be mentally sound and those that I knew were due to be released within a year. The inmates who remained were guys who were facing life sentences. The numbers I gave them were the ages that I reasoned would be the ages that, if they were convicted and sentenced to the remainder of their lives behind bars, they would decide that suicide was a viable option. For a youth of nineteen, forever is the time he waited from his eighteenth birthday to turn nineteen. The thought of spending life on the inside will settle in after his appeals are exhausted, when all hope of a release is gone and the option of an exit will become an attractive option (twenty-three, thirty-seven, sixty-seven, eighty-three, and eighty-nine).

There was a gathering of officers at the gate studying folders that contained what appeared to be photographs. The officers issued orders for two SS inmates and one Brother to report to the gate. The initial presence of the officers caused alarm, and the alarm would increase as the dorm questioned why we hadn't received the *Los Angeles Times* or why we were not allowed to watch television. The dorm prepared for the worst-case scenario. The payphones would usually turn on by 9:00 a.m., but we would be deprived of that access to the outside world also. Finally an officer approached the gate alone and called for Trey. It was interesting to me that he didn't call him by his last name, as was the custom in an institutional setting, but instead called out for "Trayvon."

Trey stood at the gate with one of his soldiers, as he realized that it would be bad form for an inmate to speak with an officer alone. Trey didn't say much, but he would nod his head periodically, indicating that he understood the message being delivered.

Trey called for a junta after he finished his talk. His calm demeanor never betrayed the seriousness of what he would reveal to us. Everyone gathered at the back of the dorm and waited for the news.

The sheriffs had begun a policy where they were singling out any inmate that was a member of the East Coast Crips or the Hawaiian Gardens Gang. Trey rambled on, explaining that the singling out of those two gangs was because a member of the East Coast Crip gang had executed a correctional officer in Chino prison months prior and then slain the correctional officer's brother-in-law, an LA County Sheriff investigating a crime in the Hawaiian Gardens projects. The Sheriffs were on guard because of information they had intercepted stating that the two gangs would strike out at the sheriffs whenever the opportunity presented itself.

Trey's remedy was to use this opportunity to align with the SS to prepare for the raids and assaults that would follow. Trey left the junta in the hands of Mad Bone as he prepared us with protocols if and when an officer attacked an inmate.

Trey moved on and approached Prieto and advised him on the news that he had received and what his orders were to the Brothers.

Without any rebuttal, Prieto agreed with a handshake and an embrace. Trey's plan for all to follow him had presented him with an opportunity to lead in a time when there would be unavoidable conflict. The sheriffs possessed the sophisticated weapons and, most importantly, the authority. I hoped that I would be able to survive this ordeal and later tell the tale. I was left wondering: What was Trey's connection with the officer that relayed this information?

Whether I wanted to be a part of a crew or a loner, I had few options; as it stood, the sheriffs had declared war and, as Mad Bone said, the rules are clear. "If an inmate is attacked by an officer, be he black, brown, yellow, or white, you must come to that inmate's aid— no questions. It's the only way we will survive."

We would get word from the neighboring dorms that the Bloods, Crips, and SS would align in the event a move were made. Weeks later, word would make it to the jail that the leaders for the Mexican Mafia, BGF, and various organizations agreed to unify to fight against any aggression from the authorities in the jails and in the prisons throughout California.

The information started to come down to the dorms that the SS structure had called up the Florencia and 18th Street gangs to make the next moves in the system and the Brothers had the East Coast and the Black P Stone Bloods in line to challenge the law.

I would come to see that mendacity is a theme woven into every policy in this cloistered society. The official story behind the deaths of the peace officers would be contradicted with the story that would be revealed on the inside. What I had started to hear resonated with what I had known as being plausible in this society.

The inmate population survives on strict protocols. No one member can arbitrarily make a decision to move without approval from the leadership in his organization. No prison riot or assassination can be sanctioned without approval. If an individual or a street gang acts on their own, they will be in the dangerous position of having to answer to the leadership.

The story was made simple for anyone to understand: the correctional officer in the Chino prison was in business with the SS, a deal that had him transporting contraband into the prison. In late 2004 he failed to make a delivery and left the SS without a major source of income; the East Coast Crips had several deals turn sour with the Florencia gang; and as the story was relayed, it was possible the Crips robbed a shipment from the Florencia gangs, among other deals that never paid off. The SS leadership made a deal through the BGF to squash the debt that the East Coast Crips had if they eliminated Manuel Gonzalez, the officer in Chino.

The Crips sent one of their soldiers to do the job. A Jon Christopher Blaylock gladly accepted the assignment. He was a veteran of the system already serving a life sentence, and considering the dramatic way that he performed the assassination, it was clear that he was determined to make a statement in his violence. On January 10, 2004, Blaylock was allowed out of his cell, under the guise that he was conversing with the SS to figure out ways to best maintain peace, but instead of releasing white doves, he drove a rusty metal knife through Officer Gonzalez's chest. It was reported that he committed the act and then calmly placed the knife down, and then in a stunt that stunned the officers that watched, he said, "I did my job, now you do yours."

Jerry Ortiz was the brother-in-law of Officer Gonzalez, and the story from the Brothers was that Ortiz was in business with Gonzalez. After Gonzalez died, Ortiz began to take shipments from the Florencia and Hawaiian Garden gangs without fear of repercussions. It is said that he singled out the Hawaiian Gardens to pay a tax for Gonzalez's death. He knew that the death of Gonzalez was at the hands of Blaylock, a Crip, but he reasoned that the SS leadership was behind the approval.

On the day that Ortiz was in the Hawaiian Gardens searching for an attempted murder suspect, Luis Orozco, he was without a partner—or backup. The story has been told that he didn't want backup or, as it has been relayed, a witness as he had decided to assassinate Orozco, known on the streets to be a missile for the Hawaiian Gardens gang and often used for kamikaze-type assignments. Ortiz knew that Orozco had similar plans, and he was eager to get to him first.

On June 24, 2005, Ortiz approached a door in the Hawaiian Gardens housing projects and proceeded to question the occupants of the apartment. The assassin quickly stepped from behind the door and shot Ortiz in the head. The official report would downplay why he was searching for Orozco without a partner. The head sheriff, Lee Baca, would only say that, although it isn't normal, it isn't against policy to be on patrol alone. Orozco and Blaylock would both stand trial and await their death sentences in the California Department of Corrections.

For the remainder of my time in the LA County Jail, I would witness how the officers flirted with the possibility of confrontation. There would be the occasional officer assault because an officer would challenge an inmate. It usually played out where the inmate would be alone, returning from a legal visit or medical appointment and without support. The officers would initiate contact and the inmate would have to fight for his life. It was understood that the inmate had little chance to beat the group of officers who were equipped with handcuffs, batons, and chemical suppressants, but the inmate had to fight. For that, the inmate population maintained an armistice.

There is truth to both versions of the events surrounding the death of Gonzalez and Orozco. The one unavoidable fact is that there are two people dead.

Valez, The Unicorn

WEEKS HAD PASSED SINCE we were allowed the privilege of television, the newspaper, or other forms of access to the outside world. I didn't have a court date scheduled. The dorm had not had a lady officer work in weeks, so on the one time when we would be graced with a female officer, it was a welcomed prize that she was working the night shift. I knew that there would be a rush to proclaim this lady the wife of whoever got a smile out of her. To some, a hello could be interpreted as an acceptance to marry. I knew that the night would bring much comedy to my life.

Immediately after the last male officer finished his fawning over the lady officer, the inmate hound dogs hustled to secure a place in line to use the bathroom. Lining up to use the bathroom guaranteed you the opportunity to view the officer up close. I didn't join in the circus affair right away, but I was able to hear someone in line comment on the smell of her perfume—a comment that drew the laughter of everyone in line, as all knew that his lame attempt at winning the love of the officer was made public.

One hour had passed and the line was buzzing with energy. I could hear the grumbling of voices as everyone knew that in short time, they would have to return to their bunks so the officers could enter the dorm and conduct their security check. I was certain that people would resume the sad affair once the officers left the dorm. The tightening of my bladder was my indicator that I would inadvertently be joining the sad affair, and there was little I could do to avoid being associated with the rowdy group that had assembled. Some had even begun to pull at themselves, hoping to gain the lady's attention.

The night bathroom rules allow for more privacy than what transpires during the day. In all the dorms, at night, there exists a one-inmate-in-and-one-out policy, where one could use the sit-down toilet and one could utilize the stand-up trough urinal, but one had to exit before anyone else entered. If someone entered while the two slots were occupied, it would be proper for the original occupant to consider the individual as an enemy making a move.

I stood in line and hoped that the guy in front of me didn't waste time by asking the lady a lame question we all knew wouldn't go anywhere. Up to this point I hadn't been able to view the lady fully, so I couldn't appreciate the buzz that surrounded her presence. But once I took her in, I understood the frenzy. She was arranging her hair, and I felt as if I had interrupted a private moment. She sat with her perfect back arched with all the grace of a ballerina, but instead, she held the job of security guard. I was up next, and it was my turn to be the lame.

I was a convert to the perverted side, and I was now allowing myself to believe that her stares were meant to convey some message of desire. My thoughts had shifted into high gear as she tucked in her blouse and I imagined that she would call me to the gate and ask my opinion on the buoyancy of her breast or how the cut of her slacks played on her frame.

I knew that I had yet to do anything obscene, like some of the characters before me. I hadn't made any vulgar gestures or any corny eyewinks. I only admired her, or more accurately studied her, from a safe distance and could only hope that my inquisitive stares didn't offend. Miraculously, I made it into the bathroom without crashing into the walls.

There I stood at the disgusting urine trough with the view of a dingy tiled wall. I quickly reviewed what I had just witnessed, hoping that her vision wasn't a mirage. She was fully a woman, where it seemed that the sheriffs preferred androgyny. I had begun to question the contempt the tailor had for the female form, based in part on how frumpy the uniforms fit the officers who claimed to be female. But this lady would change my opinion of an evil conspiracy in the textile industry that I had conjured on one of my sleepless nights.

Even though I had emptied my bladder, I remained at the trough. I was in stable thought, but I flirted with the thought of approaching the gate when I exited the bathroom and starting a conversation with her. I didn't know the topic that I would lead with, but I rationalized, if she had sympathy for my sad eyes, then maybe she would entertain me. I acknowledged that my plan was not fully worked through; I just needed to see her up close.

I was ready to make my move. There I was, firm, resolute in what I was going to do once I left the trough. Before I could tuck myself back in, a raspy-voiced old hag officer came into the picture shouting the name Valez. The tone of the hag reminded me of the way someone would sound if they had consumed unfiltered cigarettes since their youth. Her skin looked the part of the aged smoker as well.

The old trucker who interrupted my moment was a crab of a character undoubtedly at the far end of her cycle of sexual potential. Compared to Valez, the trucker lacked vitality. She was of this world that I was trapped in; Valez was of the world that I desperately wanted to return to.

All the World is a Stage

MY DAYS PLAYED OUT in the same sad fashion. Periodically, I would glimpse a female officer while passing in line as I was being shuffled from the dorm to court or to an attorney visit. The dorm would be graced with a female officer to look over us throughout the night, but that tease of an interaction would prove to be a waste.

Daily, I adhered to my ritual of scanning the obituaries, praying that I would see the name of my accuser. Daily, I cursed the editor of the paper for omitting his name—five names one day, eleven the next, but never the name I needed to see in print.

The images of Hurricane Katrina would move me to tears as I saw the photo of a little boy sitting on what appeared to be the roof of a house surrounded by floodwater. The boy sat holding a teddy bear in one hand as he rested his head on the other hand. He had taken on the role of an old man with the weight of the world on his shoulders. I thought the only worry that he should have is whether he would be allowed to stay out playing after the streetlights turned on.

The dorm I was assigned to would go through several shifts in the characters. Each side would receive new leaders and I'd watch as old alliances faded away. The dorm's chemistry would go through several turns, changing from jovial to predatory with the introduction of a few inmates. Increasingly, Bloods and Hoover Gang members filled the dorm and daily they prepared to attack the Neighborhood Crips (NHCs) as they had revived the war that they had been locked in.

I would stand by as an NHC was assigned to the dorm only to leave seconds later stripped naked. This Crip was a member of the NHC crew who had participated in beatings of Bloods and Gangstas as they were alone in court movements or while housed in a dorm where the NHCs were the majority. He was fully aware of the consequences of his participation, but he chose to leave his mark on the history of tough guys that passed through the LA County Jail.

George stood out as the most physically capable out of the new inmates to the dorm. He was a member of the 52 (Five Deuce) Hoover Gang. Over the weeks, his actions would prove what I originally thought of him being too warrior-minded to let his words do the talking. The side that he was aligned with had threats on several fronts and as he would relay to me in a conversation, "Every weakness of yours is your enemy's advantage, and you'll pay for it if you slip."

There were many days when George would sit on the bunk next to me and review what looked to be the scribbles of an old senile man. Apparently, what I saw as scribbles was actually his pitch to his many female admirers out in society. As it was, he had a mailbag that bulged with letters, cards, and photographs from girlfriends—including stacks of nudes. George enjoyed his ability to attract a woman and he showed how he disregarded the badges affixed to the female officers' chests as he made his pitch to win a conversation with the women charged with securing his body within the institution. Whenever George saw that a male officer wasn't around, he pounced on the female officer. He had no fear.

I would see how George adjusted his focus from his enemies in the NHC gang to a Caucasian inmate. Sammy would make it known from the moment that he walked into the dorm that he was a proud member of one of the many Aryan gangs. In conversation with SSs and other Caucasian inmates, he took pride as he dug deep into the Nazi propaganda vault—a decision that would prove to be his most memorable of mistakes, considering that George awaited a reason to confront Sammy. George's patience would allow him to be a witness to one of Sammy's most vitriolic of speeches—Sammy would never be the same.

Sammy had the standard muscle structure of a prison veteran, accompanied with the intricate death scene tattoos throughout his arms. His coarse Viking-style beard served to set the image of a true soldier in the Aryan Brotherhood—George was not a fan.

When George fixed his ear to Sammy's rant, he would show that his fists played a principle role in his life, specifically for moments like these. Once George's eyes locked in on Sammy, he made his approach, only asking the group of Brothers that began to gather to get his back. With the first punch, it was clear that his calculation of having his hands serve him in this interaction, and not his conversation, was the right move.

George planted several closed-fisted punches to Sammy's chin, followed with a flurry of fists, elbows, and feet. A knee to the abdomen was an extra shot; then George's knee and Sammy's scrotum met violently, ending any fight that Sammy may have had, as he lay on the ground gasping for air. The SS chose not to support Sammy's campaign of White Supremacy. The remaining Caucasians elected to leave Sammy to rule his nation as the king and the subject.

Without allowing a second of dead time to pass from George's last shot to the first groan from Sammy, they began to drag Sammy's corpse to the grilled gate and promptly alerted the officers advising them that Sammy had fallen off the third-level bunk.

The response from the officer was subdued and sadly comical. Along with two other officers, the comedian of the group opened the gate to retrieve Sammy and said, "He must've fell off the bunk several times." There wouldn't be an investigation to find out who rearranged Sammy's face. The officers didn't hide their pleasure in seeing Sammy carted off as the victim.

George sat on his bunk and continued scribbling notes to his admirers. He catalogued each woman by name and ability to subsidize his lifestyle. I was left with a clear understanding that he was fully aware of the dangerous consequences of the life he chose to live. He approached each violent interaction with a verve that was usually reserved for sport championships or childbirth. This was Hoover George, unapologetically ready for action.

I would receive a visit from Frankie and a lady friend, K. K was a psychic, but she took issue with the label and the snake oil salesman association that comes with someone that makes a living utilizing extrasensory perception and mental telepathy. K had proven to me that she was capable of extraordinary mental processes. She also had proven to me that she was above satisfactory as a lover—her presence at the visit proved that she was even more competent as a friend.

K sat in the cramped visiting booth and offered to me her breast for viewing. She made the offer with her trademark girlish giggle, which stood to justify the act as being comedy, far removed from being pornographic. K cupped her breast saying that her disclosure was "like what the girl did in the movie *Midnight Express,*" and then she giggled herself into a knot. This visit was a welcome break from what I had been experiencing.

Prior to my incarceration, I sat with K in her kitchen at three in the morning, after three hours of coitus in her apartment that was sparsely decorated with trinkets from her travels. The odd placement of candles and daggers highlighted K's eclectic mind. The kerchief that she used to tickle my naked backside was pulled from one of the daggers that she kept on her bedside dresser. The grace that she employed removed any fear that K would use the dagger to inflict harm, yet the sight of weapons caused my hairs to stand.

After a satisfying time in the bedroom, I sat across K in the kitchen, sipping a colored brew that she devised to place lovers into a more relaxed state. I wanted to test K's abilities to see what the spirit world had to offer me for my journey. K agreed without protest and without hesitation.

K stared at the top left of my head as if a conversation bubble had formed to reveal my inner thoughts, occasionally squinting her eyes as if she were looking beyond her sight. Seconds had passed and I hoped my face wasn't revealing my unease with the silence. I was seconds away from calling an end to the event, to save K any embarrassment, when K calmly and with a smile said, "What did I tell you?" The words were comforting to me, and not because it was the first thing that I heard K say since we started the probe into my soul's quest for extraterrestrial connections. The phrase was often used by my deceased brother. K said it with the same pitch and the way that her lips formed a smile was in the same manner that my brother smiled.

A calm came over my mind after K delivered that phrase. My brother would use it when I would call home from reform school, considering that he had spent a significant amount of time in reform schools himself, and upon release and before I made my visit, he would warn me of the miserable world that I would endure if I continued with my delinquent ways.

K continued with her scanning of my conversation bubbles and her expressions shifted from those of a wide-eyed adolescent seeing a circus for the first time to those of a studied therapist accustomed to the story being told, and in a direct tone, K advised me that he was okay. He wasn't in pain or lost, as he was when he was alive.

Maybe K was a charlatan and swindled men out of their earnings, but what she gave me didn't require reciprocity. I had nothing to offer K at this stage of our interaction. I had already shared her bed and I was free to walk out the door. There were no promises from either one of us. No talk of what we would do next weekend or vacations in the summer—what we were doing had ended, unless we decided to do it again. I thought it was safe to accept the words for the comfort that they provided and not look for any hidden agendas from K.

We decided to enjoy each other several times again. I didn't ask for another psychic session. I was comforted by the communication that K mediated and the enthusiasm that she employed when we were horizontal. K showing me her breast at visiting was in line with the free spirit that she portrayed.

This was it for me for months. This was all I had to look forward to. I would be transferred from the East Max facility in Wayside to the Super Max facility. The officer said that my security level had been raised after I participated in the riot. I had no say in the move. I had come to realize that the same inmates that make up the old county jail in downtown or the inmates that I had been around in East Max were the same characters that I would see in Super Max. We were all captives on the same ship.

I prepared my satchel and submitted my wrist for the chains so that I could squeeze into a cramped transportation bus for the three-minute ride. I was still an inmate, and my accuser's name still had yet to appear in the obituaries.

But even amongst a sea of blue jumpsuits and the tension of war on the horizon, I often allowed myself to take breaks where I'd replay memories of all kind. Often in this mad world, I thought about how most of these characters got their starts in crime. There were guys incarcerated for petty thefts and they all seemed to inflate their chest like peacocks to prove that they were as worthy of a "tough guy" label as the guy facing life for armed robbery or murder. Where the petty thief walks around complaining about the thirty-day sentence that he received, the proper thieves in here are all occupied, working on adjustments for the life ahead.

I thought about where I stood in the hierarchy of criminals. With what I knew of the complexities of crime, the con man was at the top of the list—that is, a true con man who never pulls a pistol, but extracts his goal through an elaborate scheme. When you pull back the veils of labels, at the basic level, there is a con to every crime. If a guy is into pedophilia, he usually finds victims in people who know him, that trust him. As it is, most pedophiles have some relation of trust with their victim, and however they attained that trust, their goal is to play whatever role they need to get to their prize. A brutally disturbing analogy that I've connected is that of a pedophile's process being no different than a paper man who passes bunko checks or credit cards, but in the eyes of "proper criminals" a pedophile is the lowest.

I was viewed by my peers as a kidnapper, and I was facing life without the possibility of parole as my reward for getting caught. I was no different than the inmate accused of being a pedophile, a car thief, a murderer. That life sentence would place me forever in the category of the prisoner. Anything but a life sentence or double digits meant that I had another chance at a real life. Double digits beyond fifteen would mean that I'd be released in my mid-forties, which meant my days of being able to sling a shovel on a construction crew would be limited. I'd be relegated to the taxi driver or hotel man-servant occupation. Even that vocation would require a presentable look. If I sustained a slash from a razor to my face, it could affect my prospects at a job where my physical presence was important—one more reason for me not to allow someone to slice at my face.

These types of thoughts were what filled my free time. I even replayed my earliest memories of being exposed to crime. I remember my mother's boyfriend, Will. He and his extended family moved to California from St. Louis in the early eighties and immediately he was a fixture in our home. Whether it was his love for sports or a part of a larger plan of Will's, he began to take me to LA Dodger games. One day when returning from a game, we stopped at the grocery store. This was in the days before cell phones, so Will stopped at one of the many phone booths scattered throughout the city to get an updated grocery list from my mother. There we stood, under the florescent lights in a lightly occupied lane, and the moment that the cashier turned her head, Will shoved two packs of steaks into his pants. Will had money and would go on to pay for the other groceries, but he saw it necessary to increase his savings by not paying for two packs of steaks and now I can rationalize that he chose the steaks over the carton of milk, because of the bulkiness of the milk carton, and the steaks were a high-ticket item—this was Will, the petty thief.

I don't remember where we were returning from, but one weekend, Will and I stopped at Zody's. I used to enjoy going into Zody's because I could pick up candy, clothes, and toys under one roof—whether or not my mom allowed me to pass through the checkout line with whatever I put in the cart was not important—I knew that every time we went into Zody's I was going to get something.

Will and I walked the aisle and told me to get some shirts, and he continued on down the aisles, reviewing the tags of pants and shirts. He gently restocked the items that didn't fit his shopping list and flung the correct sizes over his shoulder. He'd have me hold T-shirts, but eventually my six-year-old frame became overloaded with textiles and within a swoop, Will had guided me into a dressing room.

With the ease of a dancer, Will propped his leg up on the chair in the cramped dressing room and folded up his bell-bottomed pant leg, revealing long nylon socks that had brace-like straps which connected to his inside belt line. Will didn't waste a second as he began to fold shirts and pants in neat, tight squares, before he tucked several garments into his socks. Once he had accomplished maximum packaging, he folded the pant down and quickly moved on to the next leg, repeating the packaging routine.

Before we exited the dressing room, Will marched in place and jumped up and down. He looked at me and with a smile said, "I got you two shirts. Let's get out of here." Will swooped up a stack of clothes that we brought into the dressing room—what I now know was a prop—and without a rush, we exited, handing the stack of clothes to the first store attendant we came across. Will dumped the clothes onto the attendant, explaining, "My son is sick, can you put these back for me?"

In that moment, unlike the time with the steaks, I had aided in a crime. I was a prop and my payment was two T-shirts. Will was a professional. I know that now. He wore a girdle every time he left the house. Boosters, bank robbers, and cat burglars wear girdles, as it allows them to toss items into their pants without worrying that they will fall to the ground. This is how the steaks didn't fall to the ground when Will lifted them from the grocery store.

I never became a thief who stole candy from markets as a kid. I'm certain by being exposed to Will's activities and being an accomplice, the seeds of arrogance and entitlement were strengthened, if they were already present.

Tookie

"My lack of fear of this barbaric methodology of death,
I rely upon my faith. It has nothing to do with machismo,
with manhood, or with some pseudo former gang street code.
This is pure faith, and predicated on my redemption.
So, therefore, I just stand strong and continue to tell you,
your audience, and the world that I am innocent and, yes,
I have been a wretched person, but I have redeemed myself.
And I say to you and all those who can listen and will listen that
redemption is tailor-made for the wretched, and that's what
I used to be… That's what I would like the world to remember me.
That's how I would like my legacy to be remembered:
as a redemptive transition, something that I believe is not
exclusive, just for the so-called sanctimonious, the elitists. And
it doesn't—is not predicated on color or race or social stratum or
one's religious background. It's accessible for everybody. That's the
beauty about it. And whether others choose to believe that I have
redeemed myself or not, I worry not, because I know and God
knows, and you can believe that all of the youths that I continue
to help, they know, too. So with that, I am grateful…
I say to you and everyone else, God bless. So take care."
—Stanley "Tookie" Williams, death row inmate

STANLEY WILLIAMS WAS FOUND guilty of several murders in South Los Angeles and was sentenced to death. He had exhausted all of his appeals and Governor Schwarzenegger refused clemency. He was one of the founding members of the Crips, a criminal street gang that has spread throughout America. He would denounce and apologize for his leadership of a movement that he says was intended to protect the community from predatory gangs and cops in the aftermath of the Watts Riot in 1969. He vehemently proclaimed his innocence.

Thousands of protestors gathered outside of San Quentin Correctional Facility to protest the execution of Stanley Williams, but at 12:35 a.m. on December 13, 2005—Williams's birthday, no less—medical personnel from the California Department of Corrections administered a lethal injection protocol that was designed to render the patient unconscious, then to stop his breathing and eventually his heart. They achieved the goal of the sentence.

I sat on my bunk in the darkened dorm. We had been denied power and the use of all sanitary facilities. The institution was on lockdown in anticipation that inmates would stage a protest or strike out at the officers. The officers that overlooked the dorm I was assigned to appeared shocked as the male voice that came over the loudspeaker announced in a sinister tone, "Tookie is dead." The voice repeated the announcement four times, with his voice trailing off each time—followed with the sadistic laughter of a group of voices. What the officers didn't know was that the Crips had planned attacks that were to take place after the lockdown was lifted and the program returned to what was considered normal. The Bloods and the SS agreed to back the Crips' decision. The officers that mocked the death of Tookie Williams served to affirm the decision to strike at the officers.

On the fifteenth of December, a group of Crips housed in several dorms throughout the Super Max facility attacked the officers that entered the dorm to count and scan the inmates. The attacks were meant to convey to the officers that although they came to the facility on their own accord, they were not guaranteed to leave. And for this statement, the entire population was forced back into darkness; visits were cancelled, the food was served hours past the scheduled time of service, and searches were conducted for hours into the middle of the night, not showing concern for the inmates that had court schedules to attend. Life was hell, but it was a part of the deal of being an inmate—a deal that you were forced into by virtue of being confined in the county jail—and there was nothing an inmate could do, aside from falling in line or risking death.

The Locksmith

"I know of no more encouraging fact than the unquestionable
ability of man to elevate his life by conscious endeavor."
—Henry David Thoreau

UNLIKE WHAT MOST WOULD believe of the confined, in
my experience, it is rare for an inmate to proclaim his
unequivocal innocence. Most of the arguments I've heard are
creative, and very plausible, and if conveyed by a counselor with
an ability to frame a narrative, the accused might stand a chance at
receiving a not-guilty verdict.

On this day I sat in a wood-paneled courtroom with an
octogenarian judge perched on high across from me—fully in
possession of his court—and prepared to hear the inventive tales
my counselor had prepared. Ron did not lack imagination, and in
his previous courtroom battles, he had proved that he didn't take
lightly the duties vested in him.

When the perfunctory witnesses raised their hands to swear an
oath of truth, I could see Ron edit himself in preparation for the
only witness that could actually affect my life: my accuser. I placed
a governor on my emotions as I sat watching this uncultured swine
continue with his "truthful testimony." I was enraged that he had yet
to fib. Surely, if Ron probed him enough, he would shake loose a lie
or at the least a truth that my accuser would prefer stayed buried. In
cross-examination Ron displayed a certain brutality to his questions.
The way he cobbled together narratives was proof positive that

he wasn't just skilled in elaborate and devious arguments, but he enjoyed having them.

Ron consistently organized the dramatic examination of my accuser, seizing the slightest opportunity when the swine would forget his position of being the victim, and without fail, he made a mistake, and was now cornered and in a forced position where he would have to answer truthfully to a question that had nothing to do with the crime that he claimed to be a victim of—but he was on the stand.

Ron's questions were meant to serve as collateral damage and allow for other worlds to be explored. The questioning would cease at the direction of the counsel for my accuser. All sides, including the district attorney, had come to understand that my accuser would not be the most reliable witness if we proceeded to trial. There would be a compromise; I would have a chance to live.

If I proceeded to trial, there would have to be a willing suspension of disbelief on the part of the jury members in order for me to be handed a not-guilty verdict on all the charges. Ron was adept at his ability to infuse a semblance of truth into a fantastic tale, but the question remained: Would the jury suspend all judgment?

I sat in the holding cell, waiting for the last transportation bus to escort me back to the Super Max facility at Wayside. I couldn't stop playing out my options to their logical ends. I knew that there would be a point when I would tire myself and crave sleep, or so I hoped. Before I could create a makeshift bed, a trumpet sound rang out. I hurried to adjust my eyes, see what was causing the noise. The holding cell was being entertained by an Orpheus type of man, who walked the tiny cell with a manufactured trumpet—an accomplishment that was created by weaving plastic through the teeth of a hand comb. He adjusted the modified comb to his mouth and blew a tune that could compete with any brass band in or out of a jail facility.

The Orpheus song selection showcased how aware he was of his audience, as he wailed tunes that had the ability to lull the mind.

After having just done battle in the courtroom, a soothing tune served me well. I lay against the concrete wall and, for the first time, relieved myself of the burden of thought.

I arrived back to my dorm past the time for lights out. The officer permitted inmates that returned from court late to use the facilities and to adjust one's property in the common area of the dayroom, in order to avoid disturbing anyone who slept. I put to use the authority to have free range during the night hours by attempting to place a call, but unfortunately, I would be disappointed to find that the phones had been turned off. There was word that the Crips would make an attempt on an officer and for that the facility was placed on a modified program. All calls and visits were cancelled; only court movement would take place.

I received the news as an invitation to chase the vision of Valez that was locked in my thoughts. I had allowed myself to play through scenarios with her and I was able to pause the moment as I carried on with real-life activities throughout the day. But whenever I had a second to myself, I would resume the world I enjoyed in my thoughts. Oddly, the old man who slept next to me had a dithyramb-like hum and shake to his leg that would serve as the score to the pornographic thoughts that I was participating in with Valez. The occasional visit from a female friend, and the memory of my day with Valez, was the only pleasure I could hold onto. I had come to expect little from this world, and it was serving me well.

"Had I known, I would've been a locksmith," was a quote that M attributed to Albert Einstein in one of her letters. I laughed at the absurdity of Einstein entertaining the idea that he could've become a locksmith versus the vocation that he ultimately excelled in. I knew if I had chosen the simplistic job of a locksmith, life would've been presented in a more unified form, where I would've allowed myself little room for creativity. Being a locksmith is a solitary craft. A craft that I should've pursued, because having the knowledge of a locksmith would've been useful in my escape.

ACE

"A comedy to those that think, a tragedy to those who feel."
—Horace Walpole

ACE WAS THE SELF-ELECTED spokesman for the Brothers. He proved himself exactly what I judged him to be: a loud, brash, petty tyrant who gave in to every primal urge. He took much pride in his membership with the Harlem Crip gang. Sadly, he had grown accustomed to displays of anger that often played out in theatrical squabbles where Ace would choose his victim based upon their size and ability to withstand his mediocre fighting skills.

He loved to hear his own voice and jumped at the opportunity to hold a junta so he could issue edicts on trivial issues. Not having anything new, he reverted to the recycling of stale orders. Often he would use the junta as a ruse to lure into the circle an unsuspecting enemy, who was without backup. So, like the juntas I was a part of in the East Max facility, I knew that one could be made into a victim. I chose to linger in the back and simply audit the debate and remain silent.

I sensed that Ace took issue with my refusal to participate in the incessant call-and-response that he delivered at the end of the junta and as he and his group erupted with their sad display of chauvinism. My refusal to join was met with stares and I recognized that he was not pleased. He especially grew angry when he interpreted my random laughs to be at the expense of his facial twitch. At some point I would get the opportunity to test Ace's fighting abilities.

When he came to speak with me, I was quick to express my dislike for his silly antics in the calmest tone that I held in my arsenal. I hoped he would respond with violence, but he didn't. I never allowed a frown to come to my face, nor did I look at him through a sideways glance.

I faced him head on. He would be the one to turn away.

In an attempt to save face, and because he had little bravery outside of his army, he laughed at my comment. Ace put his fist out to give me a fist bump, but I refused his false camaraderie altogether, leaving nowhere for him to go but to declare war against me.

I awaited the opportunity to place Ace in his place as the thieving bully that I believed him to be. I had witnessed Ace goad lesser inmates into an argument, merely to challenge them to a fight, where he would enlist the support of his gang to pile on the lone warrior. It usually played out the same each time: they would destroy the victim and in quick order, separate him from his property. In my appraisal, these were ignoble moves, perpetrated by a petty man who clearly had no capacity to think ahead, to imagine the consequences of his actions.

That night, Ace would deliver his benediction with a preacher's fervor. He disappeared into the character of the war general, and before he finished his speech, I could sense, rather than actually see, that I was being advanced upon. Without contemplation, I pivoted to my right and issued a stiff left-hand punch directly at the soldier's solar plexus. The would-be attacker lowered his head and I followed with a right hook to his temple, rendering him obsolete.

The entire dorm looked on, knowing that Ace's plan had failed. Ace stood at his pulpit, indignant that I would have the insolence to stand up to his authority. I chose not to continue with a more detailed beating of my would-be attacker, and without much rush, I returned to my bunk and sat, waiting for Ace to challenge me.

Ace sent an older Blood to place me at ease with a tale that the soldier was acting on his own volition and that I was not in danger.

Allowing myself a moment of arrogance, I replied, "I wasn't worried," still lying on my bunk, showing Ace that I had little fear of his army.

I reasoned that I wouldn't worry about an attack through the night, when I considered that our dorm was now under surveillance by a group of officers. The bloodied soldier sparked an investigation that didn't produce a suspect, but to the authorities, the perpetrator was still free to strike again. I would take advantage of the security detail that stood watch at the grill gate. It was the most peaceful sleep I had since my arrest.

The surveillance ended once the morning breakfast was served. The daily hustle got underway with the cleaning of the dorm by the group that was next in the rotation. Like every day before, inmates announced, "Sticks in the house," as a way to alert everyone that brooms and other cleaning supplies that could be used as a weapon have been given to the dorm by the officer for the morning cleanup. On this day, the SS drew the detail.

I kept Ace and his crew in my line of sight as they shuffled out of the way of the SS sweeping the floor. I scanned and counted and rescanned the dorm and was confident that I hadn't missed anyone. Ace wouldn't allow my actions to go by, so I was prepared to take my fight to him once the morning cleanup was finished.

I waited too long.

I lost the time needed to adjust my hands to my chin, to absorb the punch coming from the side. I tucked my chin and rolled my shoulder, hoping that I had enough reflexive speed to move from the full brunt of the punch. It was apparent that I would not go unscarred, so at this stage of the battle, I only hoped that I wouldn't be rendered unconscious if the punch landed on my temple.

I pivoted away from the punches, my lead shoulder serving as my guard. Thankfully, the flurry of punches was delivered by an untrained sissified lightweight, who was more concerned with his exit from the scene than the effectiveness of his attack. He hurried up the steps to the second tier so he could view his work.

I looked up at the back of my attacker, and then I turned my attention to Ace. My anger grew as I felt a trickle of blood, followed by a steady flow of the red liquid. I was disappointed that I had allowed this coward to cut me with his punches—I now wanted revenge— but before I could fully gather myself, an officer began issuing orders for everyone to return to the bunks and then the alarm wailed. Any revenge I might be able to pursue would not happen today. My failure to eliminate Ace first allowed him to carry out an attack. The only consolation was that I remained standing and even provided a theatrical performance that may have served my reputation as a fierce soldier. I heard several bystanders comment on how I stood, studying the blood that flowed down my face—blood was a sign of entertainment in this world.

The officers removed me in handcuffs from the dorm. There was no way for me to hide the gash that stretched through my eyebrow. I chuckled at the irony in my sustaining a boxer's cut from a coward who wouldn't survive ten seconds in a ring.

I was sitting in the infirmary, waiting for transport to the LA County General Hospital, when I realized how I was allowing myself to entertain sexual thoughts of the ethnically ambiguous female officer that was in charge of the infirmary. I looked on as she sat in a swivel chair, with her khaki pants stretched tight over her wide hips. She was a thick-bodied woman who looked to be familiar to physical labor. She was far from a classic beauty that I was accustomed to admiring, but her indigenous features resembled someone from a Peruvian tribe of breeders. Under the strained circumstances, I had to view what was before me—even this lady who wore glossy lipstick that looked ripe for smearing was a participant in my ongoing fantasy.

Before the physician could add the last stitch to close the gash in my head, I had the plot for my revenge set. I just had to get back to the Super Max facility. It wasn't uncommon for the officers to shuffle bodies that have been in battles like the one I had survived.

If I refused placement in protective custody, then there would be few options as to where I could be placed. I reasoned that I would then make it back to Super Max to carry out my revenge—it might take seventeen, nineteen, possibly twenty-three days for my wound to heal; twenty-three days to prepare for revenge.

I was clear in understanding that the person I believed myself to be, and who I would have to be to survive in this war zone, would be reconciled sometime in the future. I had donned my mask and was fully prepared to act out the part of the brute. I admit that there wasn't much difference between the character I would play and the person that I really knew myself to be. I merely found it relaxing to remove my mask when the character wasn't needed. I had chosen my role carefully in the past, calling up the character to play the more violent version of myself when needed. The ability to embrace that character would serve me well in this hyper-violent society.

I worked at making up stories to deny my supporters any knowledge of the world that I placed myself in. As a juvenile delinquent, I had placed my mother in far too many situations where she was pleading for another chance from some principal, truancy officer, or judge. Azline had a raging bull to deal with from birth. As she told the tale, I decided that I wanted some excitement and refused to wait for the hospital, and instead I decided to make my world debut in the back of the ambulance with firefighters and police officers as witnesses—she knew that I would always have excitement around me, but I don't think she ever envisioned that I would pursue a career in crime.

I couldn't call my mother. I didn't want to burden anyone. I demanded that she not show up to any of my court hearings. The pressure of the world that I had joined was too much for anyone to handle, and the thought that my mother would be stressed by seeing me guided into court in handcuffs and a dingy blue jumpsuit was an added pressure that I didn't want. I knew that this journey was mine to endure—preferably, alone. I knew that controlling the information that she received would be the only way to assert control over my life, and I hoped that it would be the humane approach to dealing with my mother, even if I had to lie.

New Year's 2006

Payback

"No man can do what he knows is wrong, until he has first convinced himself that he is right." —Plato

I WAS MADE TO stay in the downtown county jail lockup until my stitches were removed. The only benefit was that I had the privilege of using the collect phone in the cell to reach out to friends as they celebrated the New Year. I only hoped my call from hell didn't ruin anyone's joy. I was certain that L wouldn't answer—and as expected, she didn't.

Another day had passed, and the calendar turned on 2005. I had survived an arrest where a squad of US Marshalls drew their weapons on me, several nerve-bending standoffs with the SS, and one major melee. I had dispatched a would-be attacker, and then the next day I became a victim to hubris. Life for me moving forward would be catalogued as before my arrest and after. All of my problems before my arrest were minor in comparison to the most minor of problems after. This place seemed to magnify a problem.

Aside from the looming trial that would determine if I would experience the world outside of these concrete walls, the only thing that filled my mind was how I desperately awaited the sight of Ace or any member of his crew. I often found myself stuck in thought with clenched fists, hoping in my next encounter that there would be enough time for me to put on a proper performance.

The gang coordinators interviewed me and were shocked when I refused to name a suspect and rejected all forms of protection; they had little choice but to allow me to return to the Super Max facility. I had sat in the downtown lockup for two weeks and devised several scenarios where I would come into contact with Ace. The situation that would allow the two of us the most freedom to clash would be if I were returned to the dorm that I had left, or if we were placed in another dorm together.

A surprise visit from M would provide me with the opportunity to exact my revenge. I was called to report to the visit late, which allowed me to view all the inmates who were already seated, locked into their conversations. My attacker sat in a visiting booth, unaware that I was passing him on the right. I tapped him on the shoulder as I continued to walk to my booth. He turned, but missed me on the right. He shrugged his head into his shoulders like a turtle, not knowing if he was going to be made a victim. He turned his head to the left, and finally he noticed that I had returned.

I noticed that he had a new chevron formation of hair sitting on his top lip. I would've laughed if I weren't in the mindset of war. The mustache was a poor excuse for a disguise and it served to highlight how ridiculous he really was. He was a petty man-child in search of an identity. The identity I saw fit for him to have affixed to his name was victim. If he ran, it would be career suicide for him, so he had to face me.

I sat in the booth and thanked M for the visit. I advised her that if I didn't call her once I returned to the dorm, then she should contact my attorney and have him call the institution to see if I was in lockup. If the opportunity to strike my assailant came and I was in the line of sight of officers, I would be going to the hole for assault. My only concern was being able to contain my eagerness to perform and not being able to stop once I started.

M knew it would be inappropriate for her to advise me against attacking, so in true M fashion, she said, "Be sure not to let him scratch your face," as she adjusted her face to a playful frown. Then we continued the conversation in a completely different direction. M had news for me from my attorney. "The district attorney wanted to negotiate a plea bargain." That news meant that I would live outside of these prison walls.

We scored several victories at the preliminary hearing. Ron managed to have the charge of kidnap for ransom dismissed. That offense alone carried a penalty of life without the possibility of parole. After court, he told me that we now had a fighting chance but not to celebrate yet.

M knew that I had other things on my mind. My interest in the visit was being betrayed by the throbbing of my pulse visible in my temple. M appeared excited at the possibility that I would be doing battle. She began to make breathing noises as she punched at the air with her tiny fist.

The visit ended and M forgave me for not being fully present. We parted ways with our hands to the window, but she was sure to meet my open palm with her clenched fist, saying with all sincerity, "Kick his ass." I hurried to exit the visiting room and take the long walk down the sparsely guarded hallway with my target. He knew that I was close behind him, and in an act to show that he wasn't afraid, he turned to face me. I didn't have issue with attacking him from the rear, but now that he faced me, it removed any backlash that could come my way for attacking him from behind. These were the rules of the gang, which only applied as it fit their position, considering they didn't have issue when he had attacked me from behind.

I didn't allow a beat to pass between seeing him turn and releasing two straight left-handed shots, which caused him to stumble and eventually attempt to flee. As he took the step to run, I grabbed his ponytail, yanking him backward and in the process exposing his jugular. In preparation for the chance that I would be in a position to use a razor blade, I began to store one in the groove of my upper lip. I was adept at retrieving the blade, and on this occasion, I put to use my carving abilities.

I chose not to cut at his jugular, but I didn't spare his face. In one motion, I tugged at his tail and brought down the blade. I made my slice and dumped the blade with the victim as I continued on the walk to my dorm. The line of people approaching from behind walked around the victim. No one stopped to assist the victim as he lay on the ground with a pool of blood filling his hands.

I made it into my dorm before the officers in the hallway noticed the victim. Seconds later, the alarms rang out. Fortunately, I had made it to the wash basin, where I was able to wash my hands of visible traces of blood. I scanned the dorm to see if anyone had identified me as the one who just sliced the bleeding man in the hallway. I didn't have any of his blood evidence on my jumpsuit, and I was certain no officer saw me. I had little concern if an inmate were to inform on me, when you consider that an informant naming me would only be good to have me tossed in the hole. The informant—or the victim—would have to testify in a courtroom. I was aware of what I did and that if any inmate chose to testify, it would be viewed as the word of an opportunistic convict trying to lighten his sentence by naming a random inmate.

I retired to my bunk with a clear conscience. The spokesman for the Brothers was a Blood named Rock Bottom from the Bounty Hunter Watts gang. He gained my attention by waving his hands as he approached my bunk. Without rushing, I exited the bunk and greeted Rock Bottom with a fist bump. Rock had a perpetual nervous grin glued to his face, and he was in the habit of referring to everyone as "my nigga."

Rock Bottom nodded his head, asked if I was good. The grin was present as he advised me that the officers were coming to the dorm to conduct a body search of everyone. Rock didn't ask for details, but his grin and nodding head indicated that he knew. And that for now, I had evaded capture.

I didn't boast of my crime. Rock Bottom and other inmates would extend their hands with fist bumps as we passed in the dorm. SS inmates became more talkative with me as the days passed. I recognized that the accepting vibe was the way convicts showed that they respected me. It would've been in bad form to ask if I did it. A question of that nature would be grounds for the inmate to be disciplined. His crew would consider his questions as a chance to gain information to pass on to the authorities.

I continued to scan the obituary section of the paper, hoping to find the name of my victim. I knew that at this point his death wouldn't bring me relief, considering that he had testified at my preliminary hearing. The district attorney would use his prior testimony against me. If his death were mediated by criminal means, I would certainly be viewed as the one who placed the order. I had come to accept that a plea bargain would be the way that this affair would end for me. Now it was a matter of how long the State of California would settle for.

My opportunity to do battle with Ace would never materialize. I was told that he was aware that I had disposed of his soldier, because he knew what I was capable of meant that I would have to go for him immediately if we crossed paths. I wouldn't have the luxury to ponder whether he would come for me.

Life and Death

ON SATURDAY, FEBRUARY 24, 2006, on orders from the Mexican Mafia, the SS attacked the Brothers at the Wayside facility. The attacks followed a domino pattern, indicative of coordination from a central spokesman. The attacks would spread to the LA county downtown lockup—Men's Central Jail. The rioting would last for days, resulting in the deaths of two African American inmates, one in the downtown lockup and one at the Super Max facility in Wayside.

The dorm I was housed in had an even distribution of Brothers and SS, which caused the SS to stand down and actually feign ignorance of their orders to attack at a specific time. Rock Bottom, realizing that Brothers were under attack in other dorms, decided to show his solidarity, and without any pushback from the population, everyone turned the attention on the SS.

I was already battle-tested and prepared for violence since arriving in jail. But after I was thrust into war in the East Max facility, I maintained a high state of alert when it came to the SS. They proved to be a petulant bunch of cannibals that enjoyed their own flesh as much as the flesh of their enemies. If I didn't know it before, I had come to learn that they were not to be trusted.

The Brothers made easy work of the SS that stood to fight. The bulk of the SS were content with staying on the other end of the barricade of bunks that they had erected. Several SS left the dorm with wounds that exposed the white fleshy meat. All left the dorm relieved that help had arrived.

The Super Max facility would be segregated, with the SS in the various dorms in the 700 and 800 wings, and Brothers, Others, and any Caucasian inmates—many who preferred housing where they weren't subjected to the rules of the SS—were relegated to the remainder of the dorms in the 700 and 600 wings.

I would go to court on February 8 to accept a plea bargain on the charges of robbery in the first degree, extortion, and a special allegation of using a gun in a crime. My sentence was ten years and eight months to be served in the California Department of Corrections and Rehabilitations. I welcomed the sentence; it was proof that I would live again.

While in the court line, I noticed some inmates without shoes or clothes. The officers had stripped some dorms of all their property. The inmates that were stripped filed their grievances with their attorneys once they made it to court, hoping that their cries would cause a judge to step in and correct the inhumane treatment in the wake of the rioting.

The segregation lasted for the remainder of the time that I was housed in the county jail. I looked forward to being processed into prison as if I had won the lottery. I knew the decade-long sentence was less than what I could've received had I decided to test the mood of a fickle jury. Ten years was a welcome sentence for crimes that could've put me away for two life sentences. Ten years was acceptable for me, considering that I did everything that was listed in the indictment.

Yes, Sir

Matthew 3:13

I STOOD IN A line with thirty naked men as we awaited permission to enter a concrete building that had a sign that stated R&R above the door. I couldn't immediately decipher the meaning of R&R. I shifted my attention back to the correctional officers who stood guard over the line of naked bodies. There was an officer wearing the Chevrolet symbol of sergeant walking the line, verifying the identifying information of each inmate. Another officer wearing the bars of a lieutenant trailed behind the sergeant. He eyed the tattoos of each inmate but never made a comment.

Without much rush in the process, the line was allowed to pass through a metal detector as we entered the building, where we repeated the identifying process to an officer who stood behind a wooden countertop desk. Another officer intercepted the line and divided the group between two holding cells. On the way into the cell, an inmate that worked in the R&R stood distributing to each inmate a bag that contained bedding and the basic toiletries. R&R stood for Reception and Receiving, and the sassy lady officer who didn't seem to have an assignment, aside from pretending not to notice the flow of naked men, stated, "You have just been received in the reception center...don't expect much; you won't be here long."

I was made to prepare for the transfer to prison at 6:00 p.m., but I wouldn't actually board the LA County Jail transport bus until 6:00 a.m. the next day. Since I had spent the last year in the jail and had been a part of several transportation movements, I knew not to expect a dinner or a morning meal. So, like the veteran inmates before me that I had seen preparing snack items for the wait, I was sure to pack a bag of chocolate, candy, and fruit to sustain me while I sat waiting for the next stage of the journey.

I had spoken to several veterans of the system who advised me of the items that I wouldn't be allowed to take to prison. In the days leading up to my transfer, I traded hygiene and food items for stationery material. It was pleasing to relieve myself of the satchel that I had carried for the last year. I would finally be free of the dingy blue jumpsuit and the paper-thin slippers that served as poor excuses for shoes.

Several inmates housed in my dorm looked upon my sentence as a gift, as they were being held to answer to crimes that would call for their next three lives to be spent in some stage of confinement if convicted. My freedom would come within a decade, and to some that sounded like the distant future, but I held on to the interactions I'd had with several inmates who were barely out of their teens and refused plea bargains of seven or ten years only to return from court with sentences of twenty or twenty-five years. I knew not to test the strength of the evidence against me. In the week before I accepted the plea bargain, I witnessed two inmates receive sentences above twenty years when offers had been made in the range of five years. Both men admitted that they were guilty, just not fully guilty as charged, and they believed that they could convince the jury that because they weren't guilty as charged that they shouldn't receive the penalty; they were unsuccessful.

As a veteran advised me before I left to "catch the chain" to prison: "Don't tell anybody how much time you have. Ma'fuckas might try to fuck your date off, because he ain't ever gonna be seeing daylight again. Mind your fucking business and if a ma'fucka look like he is gonna move on you: get off first."

He was providing me with the building blocks for life in prison.

The Girl Who Never Went Wild

I WAS CALLED TO a meeting at my friend Tony's restaurant. It was under construction and concrete had just been laid, and a dust layer blanketed the place like the smog over Hollywood. The windows to the restaurant were covered with brown paper, which didn't allow in much light during the day, and at night the construction fog lights served to illuminate the cold concrete space. Outlines of bodies and tables that were stacked with construction equipment played on the walls like shadow puppets. I shared the space with Tony, a Brooklyn boy who had made a life for himself in a variety of endeavors.

Another friend of mine, Alex, came along. Alex was Russian and upon coming to America, he landed in New York. Like many of the ambitious characters that fled the Soviet Union of the early eighties, he had visions of success in mind. He even placed a tattoo of Lady Liberty on his arm to show his appreciation.

After the preliminary hellos, Tony got right into the issue at hand. An "associate" of Alex and Tony had a friend whose daughter found herself at a party of Joe Francis, founder of the *Girls Gone Wild* video series that in 2003 played late-night infomercials on cable in a constant loop. Joe Francis was famous for hosting parties at bars in college towns known for being spring break destination spots. Rumors had surrounded Joe's aggressive behavior for years. The anonymous "Girl Gone Wild" voluntarily flashing her breasts to the cameras in a bar full of people is a situation that is ripe for someone to hurl accusations, but in this situation, there was now a name and a family attached to the breasts that he had placed on film.

I sat, listening to a story of a girl who was days into her eighteenth year of life, who had been given beer and hard alcohol, and who eventually got separated from her group of friends. The girl confessed to her father that she tried marijuana after being intimidated by Joe, who, by her first inhalation of the joint, had already moved on to cocaine. The girl confessed that by the time she woke the next morning, she was no longer a virgin and the hotel room that she had voluntarily walked into the night before now looked like a tornado had moved through it, displacing every piece of furniture. The blanket that she was wrapped in covered her naked body and there was a camera that sat on a tripod in the corner of the room.

Prior to the meeting with Alex and Tony, I didn't have an opinion on Joe Francis. I didn't spend much time concerning myself with the affairs of others, though I had heard stories of his drug-filled exploits. Our paths had crossed in business and whenever he placed a bet with me. I had been given Joe as a client from Matty "The Horse" Ianniello, an associate of mine who handed me responsibility for his gambling books, an operation I ran for years without a missed payment. I first met Matty through my boss Puggy Zeichick, who taught me the gambling and loan-sharking trades. Even after Puggy retired to Las Vegas, he maintained the books for Matty, and with my tending to the day-to-day business, our client list had grown to include less desirable clients like Joe.

And I knew that once I received the details of Joe's alleged transgressions, if I didn't step in when I did, then the team that Tony or Alex would have to bring in wouldn't take into consideration my gambling ties to Joe; but, on this occasion, he advised me to get creative in the way that Joe had become known—with a video camera and a cheesy line, "I'm Joe Francis and I'm a girl gone wild."

Coming from Matty, who at the time was the acting boss of the Genovese family, and who had enjoyed the financial benefits of the porn industry going back to the seventies, when he helped put together the successful adult film *Deep Throat*, I figured he had given me an opportunity to express my dark comedy, and that Joe had unknowingly been given another chance at life.

On January 21, a Wednesday night, I stationed two confederates at a nightclub I knew Joe frequented. Their job was to radio in to me that he had arrived and when he was leaving. I knew that Joe was leaving for Mexico the next day and that he wouldn't bring a date home, so tonight was the perfect night when I knew enough of his schedule that I was confident that I would have him to myself, without a witness.

A week prior, I had an associate who was a locksmith pose as a maintenance man, and he was able to enter Joe's mansion in Bel Air. Once on the inside, he duplicated a key for a side door.

The mansion sat at the top of a hill at the corner of Bel Air Road and Bel Air Place. Gaining entry to the home required more than the key and knowledge of Joe's whereabouts; I would have to avoid detection by the Bel Air community security, the neighbor's private security details, and Joe's alarm system; for that, I employed the assistance of an associate who had an inside track with the home security company that provided services to many homes in Bel Air.

By 9:00 p.m., I had been in the home for enough time that I had recovered video files and made copies of business documents I believed might be helpful in the future. Joe entered his mansion around 11:00 p.m., and without losing the element of surprise, I tossed a flash grenade and seized the second that I had to place handcuffs on him, effectively rendering him my captive.

For the next two hours, I placed Joe in compromising positions and had him deliver lines to a video camera that resembled the words that he had co-eds repeat in order to get a tank top from him: "I'm Joe Francis. I'm a boy gone wild, and I like it up the ass."

For that act of vengeance, I would surrender the next nine years of my life.

I tried not to spend too much time wondering what would've become of Joe had I not been engaged. Hypotheticals are best left for the conspiracy stage, not inside a prison cell. But on a call to Matty, he relayed a message that Puggy had shared. After clearing his voice to imitate Puggy, Matty explained the hypothetical that allowed me to abandon future what-ifs: "He wouldn't have heard them coming. Only if the squad would've fucked up would he have been able to hear the hammering of the firing pin before it all went dark."

CDC

I SAT ACROSS THE table from the R&R lieutenant charged with interviewing new arrivals and placing an inmate in a cell or in an open dormitory, based on the inmate's sentence and security needs. I was unsure where I would fall in the security structure, when I considered the range of inmates that shared the holding cell with me. One inmate was a third striker serving twenty-five to life for receiving stolen property—a lawn mower—and there were two inmates that I overheard talking say that they both had two life sentences. But, there also were four inmates that had sentences less than two years, so the swing in the sentences didn't allow for me to gauge where I would be housed.

I would later find out that because I had a release date that was many years into the future, because of the serious nature of my commitment offense, and because of my extensive juvenile arrest history, I would be placed in a cell for a more secured housing than the open dormitory setting until a case worker could do a more thorough review.

I heard an officer refer to me as "sir" several times and I began to wonder if I had been placed in a university instead of a prison. The level of respect that the correctional officers were extending was foreign to what I had just experienced for the year that I was incarcerated in the LA County Jail. The officers even went as far as placing a smile on their faces and nodding respectfully as I passed their post. The LA County Jail had made me lower my standards of what to expect in the way of proper interaction with men, to the point that I was now questioning the intent of the officers I encountered.

The officer that escorted the group to the housing unit stopped the movement before entering the building and questioned the group, like a flight attendant assigned to the first-class cabin. "Excuse me, if anyone is a Southerner, Bulldog, White Prider, Nazi Lowrider, or a Skinhead, then please advise me now, because you can't enter this building. There are Crips and Bloods and Northerners assigned in this building and it would be suicide for you to try and program in their turf." There were several Caucasian inmates in the line who the officer focused his attention on as he delivered his warning, and they all responded to him, that they did not belong to any of the white separatist groups, nor were they aligned with the Southern Hispanic gangs barred from the building.

After the officer issued his warning and received answers, he then turned his attention to me and asked if I was okay with the restrictions on the building. I had grown accustomed to officers and inmates checking with me to see if I was a Hispanic gang member because of how ethnically ambiguous I appeared and my choice of wearing a shaved head. I made it clear to the officer and any inmate in line that I was aligned with the Others and not any Hispanic gang—North or South.

Prior to the group entering the building, I heard another officer in the building instruct the inmates to clear the floor and return to their cells. But within seconds of the announcement, an alarm rang out, and the escort officer shouted to the officer that watched over the building from the panoptical tower to cover the group so that he could respond to the alarm at the neighboring building. The officer in the tower had his Mini-14 rifle in hand as he directed the movement to prone out as we had been told to.

And there we lay, flat on our stomachs, in the prone position. Part of the interview process that the lieutenant had conducted upon arrival in the R&R was what inmates were required to do if an alarm sounded, and going to the ground and placing your stomach to the ground was stressed as the position to be in to stay clear of the officers responding to an alarm. During the interview, the lieutenant made it a point to draw my attention to a sign that I would see throughout the institution: "There are no Warning Shots!" The warning was repeated in Spanish also: "*Aviso! Sin Aviso!*"

The officer returned to escort the group into the unit. The officer was tugging at his utility belt as he checked his canisters that contained the irritants that were meant to stop a noncompliant inmate. There was a constant stream of sweat dripping from the bald head of the officer, and with the ease of a magician, he retrieved a rag from one of the zipped pockets and cleared his head, never missing a word in his rehearsed speech, and with the flare of a big-top ringmaster, he opened the doors to the unit and opened his arms for the movement to enter.

The unit was empty of inmates, and instead of being approached by a welcoming committee of inmates in the way that is depicted in films, the officers placed a color-coded tag onto a slot at the cell door indicating an inmate's gang or ethnic association. I received the yellow tag, indicating that I was associated with Others, which meant that I didn't have to seek out my group. But they would soon come to me and give me the rules.

I headed to my assigned cell, the inmates watching the movement of the new arrivals from every window. The blue tags were for African Americans that were Crips, Bloods, or Nonaffiliated. White was for Caucasian inmates, and the red tag was for the Northern Hispanics (the Norteños). In other units, the SS would be identified with orange tags.

I was assigned to a cell on the second tier, and upon ascending the stairs I noticed that my cellmate was posted in the window, eyeing the group like all the other cells in the unit. I held the yellow tag at an angle so that anyone could see, and as I stopped at the cell, my new cellmate asked through the crack in the door what my affiliation was. I understood why he was asking who I was affiliated with, because the classification of Other can encompass many groups and some don't associate with the wider Other group; like the American Indians are classified as Other, but they stay to themselves, and some Hispanics from Central America that are technically other than Mexican but choose, or rather unknowingly align, with the Paisas, which too often are aligned with the SS.

I advised the cellmate that I was a Cuban and associated with the Others. He seemed pleased and asked if I was a lifer. I replied that I wasn't and he appeared confused. Then the officer in the tower buzzed the cell door. My new cellmate assisted me with the mattress that was at the cell. I stepped in and we exchanged handshakes and he said his name was Lee. I returned the introduction with a simple one of my own, telling Lee that I was simply called Cuba. That had become the name that everyone started referring to me as and I didn't object, and considering that it wasn't a derogatory or overused handle, I took on the name.

Lee was a Cambodian from LA and I would later find out that he was from the Tiny Rascal Gangs Long Beach clique. Lee had been sentenced to life in prison plus fifty-two years for a murder. He had also been housed in the East and Super Max facility of Wayside at the times that I was there, and through the course of the day, we would find many people in common that we served time with.

It was comforting to know that we shared association with certain people. And it would be more pleasing that Lee knew of my participation in several riots and my skillset with a knife. I sensed that he was pleased to be cellmates with someone that he believed could defend him and the cell.

Lee would go on to tell me that he was confident that he would be victorious on appeal, but he was prepared to ride out the sentence for a crime that he says was actually perpetrated by his homeboy. Lee knew that he couldn't reveal too many details, so he would let most of his revelations trail off with a comforting, "Trust me…you will see."

Lee also would advise me that the unit I was assigned to was a reception unit for inmates that had been deemed violent and/or were with sentences of life. Some of the inmates had the unfortunate burden of waking up every morning knowing that they had to serve the remainder of this life before they could start on the next life term. This explained Lee's confusion at the cell door. When I answered no to being a lifer, he was left wondering how violent I was to be assigned to this unit.

Lee and I swapped war stories from Wayside before moving into the rules that govern prison life. The biggest difference in the prison structure from what existed in the county jail was with our group's association with the various groups. In the county jail, the Others were forced to align with the Brothers, mainly because our group didn't have the numbers to stand alone. In prison, the Others remained the smallest group, but we were able to draw from other county jails throughout California, which allowed for us to maintain a group of sixty soldiers on a yard where the closest group to ours in size had upward of two hundred. It was not uncommon to find the Brothers and SS with a minimum of six hundred soldiers apiece.

Because of the Others' position of being neutral in most gang and racial affairs, we were able to deal in business with any group, and as Lee advised me, the opposing groups enlisted our services to procure certain goods they were prohibited from securing from their "enemy."

As the nights went on, I would also find out that Lee had served several prison terms for drug-related crimes. He would confess and show paperwork to prove that he also served a prison term for assaulting a rival gang while at a pool hall. Lee shared the information of his violent past as a way to make me aware that he too was willing and capable of producing damage. I wasn't sure if he believed that his thin frame was convincing to me that he could cause much damage without a firearm, and he continued with the stories of his heroic acts.

Lee gave me the program schedule from the beginning of the morning until the end of night. I soon realized that being in a cell was comforting in that I felt secure from an outside attack, but because inmates were housed in cells, the reception center was more restrictive than life was when I was in Super Max. Lee made it clear that once we were transferred to a regular programming facility, we would find that life moves on, even when you are walking the concrete yard.

I exited the cell after Lee and followed the inmates in the cell next door down the stairs to wait in the line that had formed, where inmates waited to receive the morning meal on thick plastic trays. I immediately noticed that the portions of food were triple the amount that I had received in the county jail, and surprisingly, the quality of the food was comparable to what is served at a roadside diner. The inmates that stood in line all appeared eager to get this morning meal of waffles with warm syrup.

I knew that I was in a different place than what I had endured while in the county jail when I saw the steam rising from the meal. In the county, the closest I came to seeing steam rise from food was when an inmate placed his food in a plastic bag and submerged it in the hot water that came from the coffee dispenser.

The unit was made up of Norteños and Brothers, and a limited amount of Caucasian inmates, and contrary to what I had just experienced in the county jail, the mood of the unit was relaxed with a frat-boy vibe to the activities of the inmates. Lee went into detail—in case I wasn't aware—as to why the Brothers and Norteños had such a rapport. I didn't cut Lee off as he launched into his view of the difference of association between Mexicans from the South and those in Northern California. I considered the heated battles the Brothers and the Southerners were locked in, and it was clear that the street battles in LA between the gangs didn't correspond to Northern Mexicans.

Lee was fair in his assessment of how the Norteños and the Brothers shared the same political views going back to the sixties, as the Black Panthers extended help to the inner city and not just to the African Americans. "From that time on, in the prisons, black and brown from Northern Cal have maintained a connection." That was the simplest approach. I would begin to see over the days that I walked the unit that the bond was genuine and that it actually extended to the neighborhoods.

Lee and I shared the standard war stories of our time in society, and he was clear in his assessment of how Southern California Mexicans differed from their northern counterparts, "...these fucking Southerners are just dopeheads and they will kill each other; we just got to wait them out..."

The section of the tier that I was located in was allowed to shower on odd days for ten minutes. I was relieved that the hot water flowed every time I turned the knob. Lee and I shared the multi-head shower stall with the neighbors from both sides. It was a break from the county jail's tense vibe during showers to now see that the neighbors shared a comedic relationship, like what I had experienced in a high school locker room.

I listened as the neighbors in the cell to our right joked to the neighbors to our left that he had so much time to do that his parole officer hadn't been born yet. The shower erupted with laughter as it always did when the neighbors joked, but what I didn't realize is that the joke was a play on the truth; as it stood, the neighbor was serving a double-life sentence, and if he stayed alive into his late nineties, he might be considered for parole.

The joking continued and I would find out that the neighbors to the left also had parole dates so far into the future that their parole agents had yet to be born or were possibly still in diapers. I quickly understood that the men I was sharing showers with had chosen to laugh at their situations, where I could only cringe at the thought of spending the remainder of my life and the next in this miserable world.

Nightly, the officer called out from the watchtower with a list of inmate names and orders for inmates to report to the office to collect transportation bags. Each inmate was given a brown paper bag to load all of the hygiene and food items that would've been purchased in the time that they were housed in the reception center. Everyone hated being called for transfer on a Friday night, because that meant that they would be without their personal items over the weekend and completely reliant on the generosity of their crew.

My name was called to report to the office to collect my bag, and I knew that the few items that I had collected would be out of my possession for the next days. I'd sit in my cell with Lee as my only form of entertainment, waiting for Monday to arrive when I would be transferred to Corcoran State Prison.

Lee was surprised that I was being transferred to the prison where I would serve my time so soon after being sentenced. I had just recently arrived in the reception center, and he contributed the transfer to my short-time status. I would've laughed at the comment, but I had to remember that his perspective was different than mine. I had ten years to serve, but he and my neighbors had life sentences behind their names, so I knew it was best to reserve my comments. Lee sat sipping his homemade wine and confessed to me that he knew that he "may only leave this place horizontally."

I didn't know if I'd be able to make contact with my mother or M anytime soon and Lee gave me two stamped envelopes and I wrote two letters. In the letters I hoped to convey a sense of calm and acceptance of the journey before me. An outright lie and lying by omission were fair game as they related to my mother. Even if I were facing death, I knew that in a letter or a phone call I would maintain comfort in my voice. If I begged and pleaded for help from the outside world, there wouldn't be anything that they could do to help, so going into the details of the hell hole that I was trapped in would only help in sending my mother to the emergency room.

The prime number counting that I had employed as a delinquent and for the year that I was in the county jail had come to an end. I had used the bean counting for a time that I needed to escape from uncertainty. I now knew that I had a future outside of the walls that I was locked in. I didn't know what each year would bring in the way of details, but, with prisons being places replete with schedules that revolve around inmate counts, meal times, and mail delivery, there was the possibility that I could look forward to certain moments even with the occasional eruption of violence.

I asked Lee for one more stamp, which he generously supplied, so that I could send the letter that I had written but never sent to Walter. I reviewed the letter one last time.

Dear Walt,

"What is real?" asked the Rabbit one day. "Real isn't how you are made," said the Skin Horse. "It's a thing that happens to you." And the Skin Horse goes on to say, "When you are real, you don't mind being hurt."

Walt, you know this story; you read it to me and gave me the book. It's something we discussed—what is real and what some may want you to believe is real. You've talked about Johnnie Walker being your "truth serum" and I made sure to listen to you when you went for your fourth drink—often, I prepared the drink for you—and out would come your true feelings about family and commitment, what a man is supposed to do to provide for his family—as you would say, to show them what is real and what is make believe. I'm rambling.

I'll keep it brief: thank you for showing me what is real.

Love,

Riley

Corcoran

"I'm a gangster, woman."—Charles Manson

B UILT ON LAND THAT was once home to the Tulare Lake, which fed the Yokut Native Americans for years, now sits the fenced-in perimeter of California State Prison, Corcoran. I arrived at the razor-wire-lined fence along with ten other inmates on a transportation bus. I would've been able to admire the upgrade in transportation from the dilapidated LA County Jail bus, but the Department of Corrections saw it proper to outfit the rear of the bus with a cage, where an armed officer sat looking over the occupants from behind.

The armed guards reminded us that movement, or anyone talking or looking around too much, was asking for their attention, and as the guard stated, "You don't want attention from a shaky-handed officer in stuffy quarters who is holding a rusty rifle."

An officer who weighed upward of 350 pounds stood at the front of the bus calling for inmates to report in order to have the leg restraints removed before walking down the tight path of steps on the exit of the bus. The officer struggled with each breath he took as he moved at a snail's pace. Several officers exchanged insults with him to lighten the mood, but the overweight officer didn't let the barbs derail him from his mission.

I followed the line of inmates as we assembled at the entrance to R&R. There was the waiting lieutenant that stood at the door with a file in his hand, who called for me to step out of line. I didn't know what to make of the order, but I complied. The lieutenant didn't look to be anticipating a problem with my arrival to the degree that he would need assistance from other officers, and as I approached him, he simply told me to step into an empty cell that he had opened. He locked the cell behind me and said he would return.

The other inmates that were on the transportation bus with me filed into another cell. An Asian inmate that served as a porter walked to the cells and asked everyone their shoe and clothing sizes. He approached my cell, but the lieutenant shot out an order from his office, "He will be going to the SHU. He doesn't need mainline clothes." I didn't know what to make of the news. I knew that the SHU was reserved for inmates considered extremely violent and escape risks. I didn't believe that I had done anything recently that would qualify me for either association. Making a scene wouldn't help my situation, so I unplugged and waited for information.

The porter returned to the cell after distributing bedding to each inmate and passed to each inmate a paper bag lunch. After noticing that I had an information tag that indicated that I was associated with the Others, he leaned into the cell door and asked me what name I went by and where I was from. As an Other, he had the duty to investigate if I was a "good homeboy" or "a piece of shit," because if I was a "piece of shit," that must mean that I was either a rat or a child molester-rapist and he would be able to turn his back to me without assisting my transition into the institution.

I didn't waste any time in running off my name and the news that I had just arrived from LA County, and that I didn't know why I was being sent to the SHU. He told me his name was "P-Funk from Frisco" and asked what I was in for. Being that I couldn't get to my property where I would normally provide a representative from my crew with my paperwork that listed my charges and arrest history, I had to rely on him to believe me. He knew that if I were being sent to the SHU right after arriving at the institution, then

I must've either assaulted an officer or I was validated as a member or associate of one of the prison gangs that are not allowed to walk the mainline yards.

P-Funk became creative with the use of hand-sign language, as he asked me if I had been associated with the Nuestro Familia (NF) or the Black Guerilla Family. When I shook my head to indicate that I was not associated with either of the two, he then mouthed the words, "Are you a USO?" I suspect he chose these gangs because I had an ethnically ambiguous appearance that could allow for the viewer to categorize me as Latino, African American, or someone from the Pacific Islands. I then awaited his next question, but he was limited to what he could say in the brief moment that he was allowed to interact with the new arrivals.

I then told P-Funk that I was headed to the SHU most likely because I had a case that had a lot of media coverage and I was told in the reception center that I might be a security risk. P-Funk responded back, "Did you kill one of the Kennedys?" With that, he walked off, only to return a moment later with another brown bag lunch for me. He gave me the power fist sign across the heart and told me to stay up, as we knew that at some point, I should be released from the SHU and allowed to interact on the mainline.

Two officers came to my cell and verified my name and CDC number prior to opening the cell door. They stood behind me and directed me to step into the lieutenant's office. A chair was provided, but turned in the position that placed the back support in the front and I was told to straddle the chair and keep my hands behind my back. The two officers stood at the door while the lieutenant looked up at me over his miniature glasses.

"What did you do with the money?"

I knew he was referring to my crime, so I was able to relax. I recognized that this could be an opportunity for me to assert my individuality and maybe allow the officers to see that I too once enjoyed life, so I said with a half grin, "The lawyer got it all at the end."

The lieutenant winked his eye as he let out a laugh. I didn't know what to expect next from him, but what he eventually said as he consulted the file in his hands confused me. "Listen, I was told to send you to the PHU until they evaluate you. So, these officers will take you over there. Maybe you will see that you will want to stay in club-med…"

I didn't know exactly what he was talking about when he said I was being sent to PHU, so I nodded in agreement with his decision and without asking any questions that I believed I could get a direct answer from.

I was shackled with leg and waist irons as the officers escorted me on a golf cart to what I could see as the alpha-numeric sign on the cement building that read "4A-4B." All the buildings looked the same to me, and by the time I was shouldered off the cart, I had been given the oral history of the PHU, starting with the officers laughing at the time when inmates attacked Juan Corona and other PHU inmates years back. The officers laughed at how Sirhan was an inmate in PHU and was told that he would be transferred to a PC—protective custody—yard. He was against the transfer as he stated he was against being housed where child molesters and rapists would be. He told the administration that he would hurt an inmate if they moved him, and less than an hour after being placed on a PC yard, he was returned to the PHU pending a transfer out of the institution.

The officers were quick to advise me that I should stay in PHU as it stood. The inmates had a good program and there were only forty-something inmates, including Charles Manson and his twenty personalities. I didn't know what to think considering that the unit had the name "Protective" in it. The officer driving the cart quickly stated, "This isn't about being a PC; this is the big time. To get to this unit you are a celebrity; your crime is infamous. They don't allow prison gang-fucks or any street chump here; you would've had to kill somebody big. Who did you kill?"

The officers knew who my victim was and all the salacious details of my crime. I jokingly said, "Oh, some Kennedy."

Before I entered the building I could see a group of inmates returning to their cell. That is when I first got a look at Charles Manson's fragile frame shuffling the hallway. I knew the crimes that he was convicted of orchestrating, and I had seen the desperate attempts he had made in interviews to prove his relevance in the annals of criminal masterminds. But, here he was now, in the flesh, and I couldn't imagine him being able to hurt anyone, or himself. He was rail thin, with arms that looked like pipe cleaners. His bushy mane looked to be swallowing him. But he had the strut of a peacock, full of pride.

I was reminded of an interview he participated in where Diane Sawyer asked him questions that angered him, and he eventually responded, "I'm a gangster, woman!" She looked at him, as if she wanted to remind him how much of a little man he has always been and how he would never fulfill any master plan.

I was given a single-man cell and told by the female officer the times that the security counts would be conducted. The officer looked to be in her early twenties, and a victim of the battle of the bulge. Her large breasts couldn't be contained behind the stab-vest and the bondage straps that were meant to hold her breasts close to her body. Her uniform crinkled at the buttons, which allowed for me to see the white cotton undershirt that she wore.

The officer wore her hair pulled back in a tight bun and applied a minimum amount of makeup with a touch of fruity perfume I imagined would linger long after she had left. She leaned nervously into the side crack in the cell door and whispered to me, "If you are going to masturbate, then you will have to cover yourself when you hear the jingling keys of a female officer." I was shocked that the officer was giving me the authorization to pleasure myself and I was relieved that I could, for the first time since my incarceration, pleasure myself in a room, alone.

I was able to see that the cherubic officer name tag read "Chavez." I leaned into the crack in the cell door and asked her if she would be providing me with any Vaseline or lotion to assist me in my masturbation performance. She drew back with a look of shock at the question I had asked. I reasoned that I had asked the question in the same sensitive and low manner that she'd had in delivering me the rules to masturbation while in the cells, and I only hoped that she didn't take offense to the point of calling in her male counterparts to adjust my attitude.

Chavez allowed a beat before I saw a grin grow on her face, which coincided with her cheeks turning a bright red. She looked to her right, and I suppose she believed that any officer present was far enough down the hall, and couldn't hear her as she said, "Use your spit," before she giggled like an adolescent while she hurried away from the cell.

I took in the cell and the sad surroundings. The hallways were empty of any officers or inmates, save the one male officer who shook each cell door as he passed. I had a roll of toilet paper and the standard "fish-kit" on the metal bed frame. A plastic-covered mattress was folded in half on the metal bed frame, and two crisp white sheets and a thick wool blanket lay on top of the folded mattress. Surprisingly, the metal sink-toilet unit was clean and the water flowed from the faucet with ease. This was by far the grandest cell I had been assigned to.

I unzipped the paper jumpsuit that I was given to wear by the transportation staff, and I stood debating if I should put on the boxer shorts that were a part of my bedding. I noticed a pair of socks and a T-shirt rolled in the bedding and before I could go any further with the day, an urge came over me to enjoy myself, so without any further delay, I called up the image of Ms. Chavez and I began to imagine what it would be like to be a witness to her preparation as she stuffed herself into the khaki workpants, or as she adjusted the straps on her undergarments.

I didn't require much in the way of a visual representation for me to enjoy the private moment that I was having. Ms. Chavez's image was fresh in my mind, and her instructions on using my saliva for lubrication as an answer to my provocative question would serve me with this event and many more as the days would move on.

As the night played on and the image started to take shape of the reality that I was, for the first time, alone in a space that—for now—was mine, I began to accept my cell. The sounding off of names from the various crews that made up the SHU began to echo throughout the building. That meant that it was time for the program to come to a close and for all to adjust to the next several hours of silence.

My excitement grew as I heard the jangling of keys, an indicator that a female officer was walking the tier. I lay in my bed, knowing that there wasn't much I could offer a lady at this time of my life, and a lady officer was beyond approaching, so instead of preparing a joke or a lame question for the officer to keep her in my space, I simply reviewed the emptiness of my cell and enjoyed a laugh. Before I could get lost in the space, I noticed that Chavez's face had filled the window. She stood, looking in the cell longer than needed to conduct a count of the occupants, and then she raised her balled-up hand to the window and made a gesture as if she were milking a cow. She cracked a smile and released the same girlish giggle from earlier, and then she left.

Redemption Songs

THE SAME ROLL CALL of names and salutations rang out in the morning, in the same manner as when we went to sleep. The morning meals were delivered to the cell and for a second I felt as if I were at a dingy motel with a staff that despised their jobs. I was certain not to upset the delivery process, so I listened to their orders and followed them without deviation.

I noticed that the same menu that was present at the reception center was followed here in Corcoran. One of the officers distributing the meals doubled back and asked if I wanted extra milk. I didn't drink milk from bovine, but because of his generosity, I accepted it. He left the cell whistling a tune.

The day got underway, and with a rush, I began hearing the opening of cell doors and the screeching of shoes as they crossed the concrete. I couldn't see much from the cell that I was in, but I was able to recognize a tune that was being played on a guitar. My memory of the song wouldn't be restored fully until the little man that approached my cell began to sing the words, "Redemption songs/These songs of freedom," then I recognized the song and the man singing it; I was being serenaded by Charles Manson as he sang a country version of the Bob Marley classic.

Manson stood near my cell door and bobbed his head as he strummed his guitar, never once missing a note or breaking his gaze at me. He nodded his head as he began to walk away, but then paused to ask me, "Do you need anything, brother?"

I could've ran down a list of things I wanted, but the LA County Jail had relieved me of mistaking what I believed I needed with what I really wanted. And as Manson asked the question again, I then answered back that I didn't need anything, and he walked away, never missing a beat on his guitar, or a word of the song.

I had never put too much thought to the danger that the historical Charlie Manson posed. His crimes were nearly forty years removed from the public and from everything I had seen or heard of the guy, he was not a physical threat, but one who fancied himself as a snake charmer; someone who could get feeble minded girls and loner man-boys looking for community to do his bidding. As he stood on the other side of the metal security door, he also appeared pathetic. The raggedy stringy hair that covered his face looked to have a fresh dew of sweat. His clothes clung to his skeleton shoulders and dangled like a chain around his neckline. It would be hard to imagine that he could defend himself from an attack, let alone strike out at someone—unless he came from behind. The mythological Charlie Manson was nothing more than a skeleton that crawled out of his coffin to greet the new guy on the block.

Over the next two days I would receive visits from Manson. I'd hear his feet shuffling down the hallway and like a drifter hobo, he had his guitar slung across his shoulder, ready to play a tune in exchange for conversation. He craved interaction with someone other than the men that he'd been confined with.

On the second day of Manson's visit he had a brown bag and he walked to my door and placed it at my door. Manson looked at me as he stepped backward and nodded his head. I nodded back at him. "It's yours. Free. You don't need to worry about the basics." Manson walked away and whistled a tune that he believed added to his mystique. I couldn't readily make out the tune, but the crisp drawn-out air that he pushed through his pasty lips sounded as spoiled as what I imagined his breath smelled.

I stood at the door, not seeing any movement on the floor, and without warning the jangling sound of keys approached my cell door. I was pleasantly surprised to see Officer Chavez had stopped at my door and with ease she squatted in a bat catcher position and picked up the brown bag that stood at my door and stood, looking at me through the window.

Chavez motioned with her head for me to step back from the door and I quickly complied. Chavez unlocked the security slot in the door and pushed the brown bag through, waiting for me to grab at it. "Get the fucking bag dude, I'm not gonna hold it all day."

I responded quickly and grabbed at the bag. Chavez smiled through her biting words, and then she lowered her voice and lowered her head so that she was looking into the security tray opening in the door. "I'm going to come back and I want to see something—don't be shy."

I was definitely growing in stage fright as I looked at the lust in Chavez's eyes and the rasp that overcame her voice as she whispered what I realized was her demand for me to put on a performance for her. My confusion as to who else I would be performing for consumed my thoughts; I hoped Manson wasn't going to be present. I hoped Chavez hadn't become a disciple of his and he now found pleasure in being a voyeur of new arrivals.

I quickly tore into the brown bag and dumped the contents down on the bed and was surprised to see a tube of Colgate toothpaste, a proper toothbrush, a bar of Dove soap, and a small bottle of lotion like the kind given to guests at hotels. I hoped this wasn't payment for my body. At the bottom of the bag there was a note signed CM. It was a simple, one-line note: "Life isn't over."

I didn't know how long Chavez would be gone or what I should be doing when she returned. I was already standing in the cell dressed only in my boxer shorts, so I was a hand maneuver away from being able to retrieve my desired body part from the slit opening. I just didn't want to be prepared only to have dreamed that

Chavez wanted to view my body. I was now on the tenth back-and-forth of a walk that took me three feet from the bed to the door and back, and I had yet to come to a decision.

Before I could fully bring myself to an erection, I heard the jangling of keys. I remembered that Chavez originally said that the female officers will jangle their keys when walking the tier as a way to warn inmates that a woman could look in the window, as a way for the inmates to cover themselves. So there I stood, rapidly pulling at myself in hopes that I could achieve a proper erection for whoever it was that would be looking into my cell window.

I noticed that the keys stopped jangling for several seconds before the sound of combat boots started up and increasing with intensity. I reasoned that the booted person was within two doors from being at my cell door and I was well on my way to a full erection and either an approving wink from Chavez or a beatdown from an officer who had no interest in my performance.

I stood a foot away from the cell door, which allowed me to hide my erection from whoever looked in the cell, but at a position where I could take another step back and fulfill what I believed to be Chavez's desire to survey the new goods on the cellblock. I was committed to a performance of some kind, and as the jangling keys stopped at my cell, I was relieved to see Chavez's round face filling the window. Chavez paused at the window and her elevator eyes were my cue to begin the show. I stepped back and lowered my boxers.

Chavez's eyebrows raised with a look of delight at what I was showing her. I followed her expressive eyes and head movements, which indicated that she wanted me to stroke myself, and I did. Chavez peeled her eyes away from me for a second as she surveyed the hallway, and quickly returned to my now fully erect penis.

I had at that point been incarcerated for over a year with little attention from a woman or the access to enjoy myself, and here I was being allowed to please myself for the entertainment of a female officer. The mix of sexual pleasure and walking on the dangerous side of an inmate-officer affair intensified my erection and I was now standing in battle mode in full view of an intrigued, albeit frustrated, Chavez.

I stepped back farther and sat on the bunk and continued the performance with gusto. Chavez's approval was evident as she was now assisting me in the act as she traced her index finger around her mouth. The implication was that she was assisting me in oral sex. I continued and Chavez never broke her gaze.

Chavez's frustration with just viewing overtook her and she was now unlocking the security slot in the cell door. Chavez lowered her head and now there was no barrier between the two of us. In a low tone, Chavez called to the door, which I quickly complied—leading with my erection. I placed myself at the slot and Chavez placed her hand in and met me with a firm grip that served as her anchor as she allowed herself to tug at me several times before reality set in and she released her grip.

Chavez quickly closed the slot and nodded her head for me to continue. All fright had left me by this point. I didn't rush as I walked back to the bunk, where I lay down and continued to enjoy myself. I lost focus and didn't care if Chavez was still viewing me as I continued with the task; a task that came to a monumental conclusion—a conclusion that pleased Chavez as she remained at the window, surveying my cleanup routine.

Chavez nodded her head with closed eyes and I took the look to be a sign of approval. I didn't know if the occasion called for me to initiate a conversation or to remain in the reclined position, naked and posing. Chavez remained at the door and I remained reclined on a paper-thin cot that was serving as my conjugal bed, the cell door serving as the prophylactic.

I imagine that Chavez's review of my naked body would serve her in the future, because I was certain that the event would be a memory that I'd be able to draw upon for the remainder of my confinement—and if I was lucky to be allowed a repeat performance, the event might stay with me beyond these walls.

I figured since Chavez remained at the door that I should say something. A thank you might be too pretentious and a come again comment might not be accepted well, so as a joke, to lighten the mood, I pretended that my ejaculation had left me speechless, and surprisingly, Chavez began to giggle. There weren't any statements by Chavez, nor did she appear embarrassed. Her command of the movements in the housing unit indicated that she had used inmates as her personal sex performers, and I was just another in a long line of studs to come through in chains.

Chavez continued with her security walk. Her keys began to jingle as an alarm to any inmate that might be in some stage of undress. My cell was at the end of the cellblock, so Chavez turned 180 degrees and was now walking back past my cell with a permanent smile to her face and not a hint of regret or shame.

I sat on my bunk and enjoyed the fresh memories. For the first time in over a year, I was graced with a woman's skin touching mine. As a confined man, sex and all avenues of sexual release are criminalized, and for the first time, I was allowed to act on sexual desires.

I was served dinner in my cell at the prescribed time. After the meal was served, Manson made his way down the tier with his guitar in hand. He played a familiar tune that set the mood of a long night to come. Manson played and sang the words to Billie Holliday's song "God Bless the Child" with a surprising smoothness to his voice. I didn't have much, but the little that I did have was all that I needed.

Manson paced the floor singing the song and he made certain to lock eyes with me as he made a pass each time, and he was sure to nod his head. Manson made his way to my door on the last pass and while standing less than two feet away, he posed an odd question: "Where is my duck?"

I didn't know what to make of his inquiry. I didn't know if duck was code for something sinister and I was in charge of his duck, but I didn't know where I would've gotten the duck from. Manson asked the question without venom in his voice and after he asked it, he continued his guitar play and picked up the song where the tune was. The expression on his face was pleasant as he sang and walked away, never returning for the night.

I lay on my bunk without much care for my current housing assignment. My experience with Chavez and the odd question from Manson provided me enough comedy for whatever was ahead. For now, I decided that there wasn't anything that I could do to change the odd interaction, and sleep would not be a thing for me. I sat up and reviewed the surroundings, and I had the urge to light up a cigar and sip a glass of bourbon or something that would burn as it went down. All I had was a dusty cup that I filled with hot water that I slowly sipped and pretended that it was an alcoholic drink—a rolled-up wad of toilet paper served as my cigar and I was far into the thought that I was in some cigar bar in a foreign land, watching the locals.

Committee

BEFORE THE MORNING MEAL was served, an officer tapped at my door and whispered through the crack in the metal that I had committee after breakfast. The officer appeared to be a fresh-faced teen, eager to be deployed to some war zone. The crew-cut hairstyle and every tool that an officer could fit on a utility belt highlighted his Boy Scout roots.

The harsh sun had beat down on the cement structure, heating the cells to one hundred degrees before 8:00 a.m., and I would remain in my boxer shorts without a shirt. The officer at the window was sizing me up. Unlike Chavez who sized inmates for the potential of having herself a mate, male officers surveyed the inmate population for potential threats, and this officer was in the midst of a thorough viewing of how I had developed my body and how I chose to use the space that I occupied.

The young officer made his announcement and instead of hopping to my feet, I decided to play out my time with Chavez, except in my illusion I decided to change the location to an exotic island resort town where I had my pick of the local girls—all of them much younger and inviting than Chavez. My imagination was my entertainment and every officer that passed my cell and every voice that I heard in the distance became characters that I could assign alternative titles to—some officers made it to hotel wait staff and others didn't make it out of the valet station as they parked the golf carts that shuttled guests around the island. I knew that I could survive this ordeal if I didn't lose my imagination nor my sense of humor.

The officer stuffed a white jumpsuit reading CDC INMATE on the back into the security slot in the cell door. The officer's tag read M. SANTOS. He stood at the cell and waited for me to dress. His nervousness grew with each second that I took before I advised him that I was ready to be retrieved.

I tapped the cell window to advise Santos that I was ready to go to the committee meeting and his rail-thin arms jutted out from his short-sleeve firmly pressed khaki shirt. His boney shoulders made his shirt appear as if it were placed on a hanger in the closet.

When waiting for the backup officer to assist Santos with my movement, I wondered if Santos was the type of guy that awaited the day that he would be old enough that his long, exaggerated face would play well as an older man. As he was, it was hard to see how he could ever be viewed as a heartthrob in the way that boy band members are desired by teen girls. A job as a correctional officer was in line with someone like Santos—he didn't seem like he ever belonged to the jocks, the rockers, the nerds, or even the loners. Being a correctional officer is a profession that could provide an outcast like Santos a side to belong to. Whether his side wanted him or not, he was on their team and I was a part of the opposition.

Two larger officers joined Santos to retrieve me from my cell and they allowed Santos to issue the orders to me to turn and place my hands through the security slot so that I could get the first of a series of chains that would be fixed to my body.

The officers continued their conversation, never allowing Santos the opportunity to add to it—a point that wasn't lost by Santos as he sighed and cleared his throat to get their attention and assistance in shackling me. I hoped Santos didn't take out his frustration on me.

For the first time since arriving at Corcoran I was freed from my cell. Granted, I was shackled with the traditional wrist bracelets attached to a waist restraint and guarded by three officers. As I surveyed the building, I noticed the officer that stood guard in the tower with his Mini-14 rifle slung across his chest. The tower guard held what is called a block gun, as it shoots block type of bullets that are categorized as nonlethal in lieu of real lethal bullets.

Santos held firm to my shoulder as he directed me to a door that Officer Chavez stood by. Chavez smiled as I approached with my escorts. The larger, balder officer issued a provocative command to Chavez, "Open the door or crack them thighs." I didn't know what to expect as a reaction from Chavez considering our interaction the day before. I was certain that if she allowed me to perform for her as I did after only interacting with me through the door, then surely a man in free society—and several of his friends—could've had his way with her.

With a devilish grin glued to her face, Chavez turned to open the door that she stood guard at. I was able to see Chavez's full body. She filled every inch of her tactical jumpsuit, and her effortless transition from sex fiend to dutiful centurion was evidence that she was well versed in the world that she was operating in.

Officer Santos directed me to sit straddle-style at the empty chair positioned at the end of a table lined with stuffy men in dingy suits. They looked like rejected literature professors whose ambitions had been drained out of them in their youth. To my right sat a bushy-haired octogenarian dressed in a corduroy jacket with leather patches on the elbows. The old-timer fidgeted with his thick-rimmed glasses, never knowing if he wanted to use the glasses or allow them to dangle by the string around his neck. He had perfected the rambling professor role.

The next two men to his right were dressed in correctional officer uniforms. The first of the two officers held the rank of lieutenant and the next officer had the double gold bars of a captain. The lieutenant embraced his male-pattern baldness and it appeared that he worked more at the chevron mustache than he did at the ring of hair that clung to the sides of his head. The captain was gifted with a full head of hair that he kept trimmed on the sides with an odd collection of tight curls that rested on the top like a bird's nest. Both men's muscular frames filled their long-sleeve shirts.

Across from me at the far end of the table was a rotund man in a tight gray suit. He wore his tie loose around his thick neck, possibly so he would be able to breathe. The two men to my left wore polo shirts and did the bulk of the talking once the proceedings got going. The first man to my left stood well over six feet five inches. He wore the look of an ex-athlete who continued to exercise at the sport that he may have excelled in while in some junior college, but an athlete whose tall tales never acknowledged that his best years ended before he finished high school.

Both men were dressed in dark-colored polo shirts with newly acquired stab-vests that hugged tight to their frames. Both men also were adorned with Asian-style tattoos, even though the men were Caucasian. The man that sat closest to me had a tattoo that indicated that he was a member of the Marine Corps. The oft-repeated Semper Fi motto of the Corps showed from under the sleeves of his shirt and once he began to talk, I could tell that he held firm to his structured life in the military.

The tall marine advised the room that he was the counselor assigned to the PHU/SHU housing unit and that he was representing my case before the committee. The assembled group was introduced by the marine and then without wasting time he turned to me and asked, "Do you want to stay in the PHU?" Without hesitation I answered, "No." The group looked at me with shock, but no one spoke up.

The marine then asked why I was denying housing in the PHU. Before I gave my answer, the marine had prepared to write it. Without a long drawn-out explanation, I said, "I don't need it." The marine rambled on the benefits of being housed in the Protective Housing Unit (PHU). Without being asked, I stated, "I don't need it."

The marine removed a paper from a file that sat on the desk in front of him, and he placed the paper in front of me. Without any more questions, the marine stated that I could sign the form that states that I'm refusing the protective housing assignment.

The lack of concern in explaining the benefits of the housing assignment was an indicator that the administration didn't care to waste time on my case, and the next step was to cover their jobs by having me sign off on a protective housing refusal form. The other men in the room never spoke. All continued reading forms that they had at the space before them. The lieutenant and the captain both awaited the moment that the committee meeting was finished. I reasoned that they looked to be anxious for the chance to make an earlier tee time at the golf course. I was just another inmate coming to serve time, and if I didn't want protection, then they were not going to force me.

The marine advised me that he would deliver the form to my cell so that I could sign off. Santos stood behind me and once the marine issued a head nod, Santos stepped behind me and gripped my arm to guide me to my feet.

I walked the hall back to my cell, and I hoped that I'd be able to overhear more banter between Chavez and any of the officers. Hearing Chavez's conversations with other people would allow me to place some context behind her hypersexual approach to her job, but Chavez remained on guard at the door. I couldn't turn to look at her. I didn't know if anyone had recognized her extended interaction at my cell door, and they awaited clues to confirm that we were involved in an affair.

I sat in my cell and wondered when I would be transferred to my new housing assignment. The marine brought the form for me to sign off on where I declared that I am not requesting protective housing. The marine advised me that I would be transferred to a Level 4 secured yard, even though my security level was determined to be adequate to be housed on a Level 3 yard. The marine said the assignment to a higher level would be so that the institution would be able to monitor me closely.

I didn't protest the Level 4 assignment. I reasoned that the same characters that would be on the Level 4 existed on the Level 3, with the inflated tough guy acts because an inmate was on a Level 4 and expected to be on the ready to perform in the most violent of situations.

I didn't get a chance to interact with Charles Manson, nor was I able to find his duck. Inmates like him need protective housing. Someone would likely find it a trophy to take a shot at him, even in his advanced age. The benefit was he got to live in an ultra-secluded society with creature comforts that were meant to pacify, but the drawback to being kept in those conditions was that the only people to interact with would be the same exact ones, day in and day out. That meant no new stories, no new people to share new experiences—just the same old men growing old in an exclusive, sterile environment.

I needed to be around people. Even if I didn't engage in conversation, having the ability to study them would satisfy curiosity, allowing me to create new stories for my enjoyment.

Staying in the protective housing unit would only be good if I were truly in need of protection—like Charles Manson, and his duck.

AVISO! SIN AVISO!

While waiting to be transferred to Level 4 yard, an inmate on the yard was shot dead by the gunner in the tower. Two inmates were attacking another inmate with a crudely fashioned knife and surprisingly, the officers actually showed restraint and initially fired the block gun at the attackers, giving them an opportunity to abandon their attack before firing with Mini-14 rifles.

One shot hit the main attacker, but his confederate continued the mission and stabbed at the victim even after the officers attacked with batons and applied their chemical agents. *AVISO! SIN AVISO!* was one of the signs that littered the prison, advising all that the warning on the wall was the only warning that you would receive.

The institution remained on lockdown for several days. The institution takes precaution after serious incidents to test the temperature of the population. An officer killing an inmate could result in the inmate's group seeking revenge, so staff would conduct searches of cells and the yard and try to round up inmate-made weapons. But at some point, inmates would be released and the institution would have to wonder when there would be retribution.

Level 4

I STOOD AT THE window of Unit 4 of A yard, Level 4. The tall, dark-skinned inmate that placed a fish-kit plastic bag at my door had repeated the title to several new arrivals. I could hear "Ice" advise inmates that they didn't have much coming until they went to committee, which, as he said, "won't be until next week, or when they want to have it."

Ice consistently started his conversations with people in the living unit that he had been "locked up for twenty-three years and ten months, and I ain't with the bull." This line was a standard coming from Ice in conversations whether it was a confrontation or a pleasant interaction. The time that Ice said he had been incarcerated seemed to be validated, and as the days went on, the time that he says he was confined had increased.

Ice came to my door and advised me that "big homies are coming to talk with [me] soon." There were only two inmates associated with the Others in the housing unit. They both worked all day and had yet to make it to interrogate me.

Ice brought to my door another bag that he said had come from my "homies." He stood at my cell door and waved to the staff in the tower, requesting that the cell be opened. The tower staff waited to see me in the window and give the thumbs-up of approval before he opened the cell door. I suspect that in the past inmates have been attacked by acting like they were friendly with the inmate in the cell and the tower staff opened the cell remotely, only to find that a group of inmates made their way into the cell to attack the inmate—my thumbs-up became the approval that he needed to open my cell.

Ice deposited the bag and we exchanged fist bumps as I thanked Ice for delivering the package. We shared basic pleasantries. Ice took great pride in his hometown of Chicago and he constantly reminded me that in his town they "do it different than the squares here in Cali." Ice had a lot to say and he was sure to say it loudly and with confidence as a way to convince himself that whatever he was saying, the recipient would buy it whole.

Ice could hold a conversation about any topic at any time and most of the talks that I overheard him engaged in he was always working a deal. Ice sold the supplies that were left over after every inmate received the weekly rations; he sold contraband radios and other items that were seized by staff, but some way ended up in his cell. Ice was the inmate to talk with if you needed an item that wasn't available. Ice repeated the time that he has been incarcerated and before he left my cell door, he casually revealed that he had a double-life sentence to serve, and he was confident that he would someday go home.

While at my cell, Ice exchanged verbal insults with a cross-dresser who called himself Michel, but whose actual name was Michael. Michel, as this confused man had called himself, wasn't satisfied with some deal that Ice was engaged in. Michel stood well over six feet and the muscular frame of a former athlete remained even though Michel had injected his body with female hormones. The stubble and the outline of a beard were evidence of a once potent testosterone-filled manly body, but the body that I was witnessing only served as a reminder that a sad, disturbed person would forever occupy the space, no matter the amount of hormones introduced.

Ice asked Michel to step to the side and that was the cue for me to close my cell door. I stepped out of the view of the window to the cell, but I continued to listen to the conversation, and within seconds I heard Ice recite the often repeated line where he advises his audience that he has been incarcerated for twenty-three years and ten months and in this instance, he followed up the timeline with a threat to Michel that he would "Fuck your shit up!" Michel didn't seemed phased by the threat and actually assumed a defensive stance in preparation for whatever offense Ice may be considering—Ice appeared lost as to how he should respond once Michel stood up to him.

Ice unleashed a volley of abusive words and scenarios by which he would harm Michel, all while Michel maintained his readiness to clash, and then Michel's mood changed from confrontational adversary to that of someone who was in possession of a secret. Michel raised his voice to the same level that Ice had been talking and he said, "Well, you wasn't talking shit when I was sucking your dick, nigga!" That revelation enraged Ice, but instead of striking out with fist, he went into a tailspin and protested vigorously, but never did he strike out at Michel.

The various inmates and officers that were lounging in the building looked on with shocked expressions at the revelation and the less-than-violent reaction by Ice as he had no response but a string of threats without action.

I had a bag of snacks and some basic rations in the bag that Ice had delivered to me, and outside my door I had a live-action telenovela performance starring Ice and Michel. I hoped Ice didn't strike out violently at Michel as a physical confrontation would put an end to the hilarious screaming match. I sat on the bunk and listened to the comedy, hoping that it would last at least for the remainder of the day. I was a new arrival to the yard and as rules dictated, new arrivals must remain on quarantine until the inmate attends a committee hearing to determine that the inmate is properly housed and that there are no threats to or from the inmate to the safety and security of the institution. The cell would be my world until I was cleared to walk the yard, and if the drama between Ice and Michel was an indicator of the craziness surrounding this building, then I would be thoroughly entertained.

Prior to the 4:30 p.m. count, a group of inmates returned from work, and a rather tall Chinese inmate stood to the side and tapped on my cell door. I quickly rose to my feet and greeted the man with a simple, "Hey, how are you?" With a clean American accent, the man on the other side of the cell door stated his name, and affiliation, and advised me that he would come back after chow, and just like that he was gone.

China Mike didn't have much room for small talk. Ice had already told me he was one of two Others on the unit—and then proceeded to ramble on about the rumors that surrounded every inmate that walked in the building when we talked. China Mike's story excited Ice, as it was folklore that China Mike had killed two undercover cops in a drug deal gone bad. It is unlikely that Ice knew the real story, but it was clear that with Ice, a good story was better than the truth.

The unit count was being conducted by a little redhead who jangled her keys in the same manner that Chavez did, but the way that this officer barked at inmates to prepare for count indicated that she wasn't interested in any nude performances. The male officer in the guard tower that overlooked the unit made an announcement over the loudspeakers for all inmates to "prepare for count" and that "a female is on the tier."

That announcement was the only warning that an inmate would receive. If an inmate exposed himself, he wouldn't have an excuse that he didn't know; even standing at the toilet to urinate was off-limits until the officer finished walking the tier by threat of a major rule violation and the possibility of sex offender status.

The count cleared and the doors began to open for the night dinner movement. A sea of inmates flowed out of the building, some using the movement as an opportunity to exchange items and lounge throughout the unit. The unit was staffed with two officers on the lower-tier floor who were virtual victims. If a group of inmates decided to strike out at them, I wondered what, if anything, a female officer like the little redhead could do to put up a defense.

China Mike returned from dinner shortly after the movement began. He made his way to my cell and his mood was more relaxed than it had been an hour earlier. When Mike introduced himself to me, he omitted the China name. He opened the conversation with an overture, wondering if I needed any rations. Mike inserted an envelope with my "paperwork" that I had Ice deliver to his cell, prior to Mike returning from work. Mike nodded his head and assured me that "everything was all good."

At this point I had passed a major hurdle, having Mike clear my paperwork of any red flags, and had the weight of the yard accepting me, which would extend to the remainder of my stay in prison if I didn't violate any of the inmate-imposed rules: don't snitch, lie, steal, or let your crew down, and don't talk to the cops. There would be more rules revealed, but the basic rules applied to all the crews in prison. Each group had rules that serve their inner political playbooks, but following the basics would increase a new arrival's chance of survival.

I didn't know the full story of what brought Mike to prison, but he looked like a man that realized that he would never be on the other side of the walls as a free man, and whoever he allowed in his life would have to be as serious as he was and ready to defend their position to the death.

The unit began to fill with inmates returning from dinner, which was a bell of sorts for Gutierrez, the redheaded officer who took pride in barking orders for inmates to return to their cells. Mike let me know that he wouldn't hang for long and if I needed him, then to send word with Ice or one of the "porters" that ran the tier. Mike clearly didn't need a friend, but he seemed to welcome someone that he recognized as a team player, and the relief that covered his face when I answered no to his question of whether I used dope of any kind let me know that he didn't have patience for the experimental types.

The next couple of days played out the same. I was confined to my cell until I attended the committee hearing so that the administration could clear me to walk the yard. I was allowed to shower daily during the morning shift. By the time Gonzalez arrived to work at 2:00 p.m., my day was finished, so I didn't have any interaction with her except listening to her sharp tongue and obnoxious tone as she issued orders to inmates.

My neighbor to the left was an older crippled Caucasian inmate who screamed back at Officer Gonzalez whenever she started issuing orders. My neighbor challenged Gonzalez even when he was in his cell. No matter Gonzalez's gripe, my neighbor would respond and end every line with his go-to line: "You sound like my wife; that's why I killed the bitch!" His words didn't affect Gonzalez, who continued her rant, never even looking in the direction of the sound.

I had been in the custody of the California Department of Corrections for nearly two months and aside from Chavez, Gonzalez was the only female officer I had seen that was directly in control of inmates. All of the male officers maintained a level of respect, the complete opposite of the sadists in the LA County Jail. In one of Ice's visits to my cell door, he commented about Gonzalez's lack of understanding of the one rule that all officers should always maintain: They go home at night because we allow them. So I wondered why Gonzalez found it necessary to be so confrontational with every inmate. I hoped if she became a victim of one of the inmates who had multiple life sentences to serve, that I was far from the area of attack.

Daily, Gonzalez's screams rang out like bullets at their targets. I was pleased to see that Michel was ready to challenge Gonzalez for the rank of "Queen Bitch" of the building. Michel took every opportunity that presented itself to advise Gonzalez that her hairstyle made her look like a wet cat or that her choice of perfume smelled like a feral animal. Michel was unrelenting, but Gonzalez worked hard to ignore Michel, only to hear commentary from other inmates who repeated Michel's insults.

Yard Dawgs

"Human action can be modified to some extent,
but human nature cannot be changed."
—Abraham Lincoln

STEPPING ONTO THE YARD for the first time was a dizzying experience. Inmates walked the track in one direction. Groups of inmates laid claim to basketball courts and huddled at tables scattered throughout the yard. A fence ran down the middle of the yard with an opening at the halfway point of the yard. The officer in the tower made the announcement over the speaker that the gate would be closing in five minutes and for inmates to pick a side. Mike had come out to the yard with me and I walked with him across the grass to a table that sat several inmates that looked to be Pacific Islanders—they rose as we approached.

Fly stepped forward and extended his hand, making the introduction for himself and the other guys in the crew. Sunny stood to Fly's right and he stepped up with his hand extended. He stood more than six five and was easily 230 pounds of solid bulk. Scars spiderwebbed his knuckles and a collection of veins ran the length of his arms, all eventually hiding themselves under his T-shirt. Sunny was a dark-skinned Islander who oddly had the accent of a cowboy, instead of the tone of a city boy who grew up in Southern California from the age of twelve when he came from the Tongan Islands. Sunny shook my hand and still managed to maintain visuals on the yard as inmates continued to fill both sides of the fence. It was clear that Sunny was security-minded.

Big Ed, who appeared to be in his late fifties, was the elder of the group and more than one hundred pounds overweight. From the moment that I got in hearing distance of the table, I could hear Ed complaining about the arthritis in his knees and hips. Even with the extra weight, Big Ed's frame was that of a midsize Sumo wrestler. Ed's handshake involved him enveloping my right hand with his right and left as he locked eyes with me while introducing himself. He quickly sat down as the arthritis pain complaints picked back up where he left off.

Shamu stepped forward next and extended his hand to meet mine. Shamu appeared to be in his mid-forties even with his paunch belly and chubby face. Shamu constantly tugged at his shirt that clung to his body at every crevice and around his neck.

Next to Shamu at the table was a feminine character who extended his hand in a manly fashion and introduced himself as Suka. Suka's eyes were hidden behind a pair of Chanel glasses meant for women. His hair was close-cropped and wavy, designed in the fashion that resembled a flapper from the 1920s. Suka's clothes fit tightly, which made me believe that he had his clothes tailored to highlight his midsection.

I didn't recoil my hand when I saw Suka stand to greet me. It was clear that he ascribed to the homosexual character, and with the strict beauty regiment that he displayed, I imagined that he had several suitors to complete his character as the "yard bitch," as he jokingly introduced himself then moved onto the inquiry of how my time in the Corcoran prison was going.

Sunny spoke directly to me, asking if I jogged, because he needed a new jogging partner. I answered yes and he said that he would get me some state shoes or some boots to run in, reasoning that there shouldn't be a problem for me to run in boots because he did it all the time.

Suka stepped into the conversation and let me know that he would see which jobs were open in the program office, because he was the captain's clerk. The group didn't seem to care that he was a homosexual. Like the Brothers, the Others didn't approach homosexual inmates the way that the Southern Mexicans and whites did, where a homosexual inmate would face immediate death.

Suka let the group know that he was going to work and issued fist bumps to everyone, and once he was out of earshot, Fly jokingly let it out, "The homie Suka been gay since the streets, but Uce is cool. He do his thang, and he don't fuck with anybody, so we don't push a line on him." Fly had the attitude of a street thug who was constantly searching for the next deal. He was shaped like me but wore a beard full of gray hair. Fly probably had fifteen years on me but his command of the hip-hop vernacular served as a bridge for Fly to stay current with a new crop of inmates that were coming into prison from the neighborhood that he once walked.

I couldn't say definitively that the group viewed me with suspicion because my speech wasn't riddled with slang terms. It was possible that Fly hoped that I would slip and speak freely and reveal a term that could indicate a region that I came from. My clear American English speech denied the group a chance to know if I was a "former" gang member and a possible threat to our group. As Sunny stated, "We have Bulldogs on the yard and if you was a Northerner, and they found out, it will get bad. Tell us now."

Every movement in this world was on display and being catalogued by multiple people. The Hispanic inmates eyed me from the moment that I arrived to the building. It was public knowledge that I was associated with the Other group, but the other crews didn't know if I was originally from Southern or Northern California and associated with either Hispanic group that was in a protracted war with the Fresno Bulldogs that were sharing the A yard with the Brothers, Woods, and the Others.

I assured Sunny and the group that I was not nor had I ever been associated with the Southerners or the Norteños. Sunny nodded his head, and without adding much to the conversation, he simply stated the group's position: "That's it, I'll let them know."

I had already been cleared by Mike so I was allowed to walk the yard without any further inquiries into my criminal profile. If I hadn't been cleared I would've had to stand on guard in an area until my crew could review my paperwork and any background information that other inmates on the yard or from other yards may know. Sunny told me as I began to walk the yard with him—at his suggestion—I had a clean slate and it was on me if I wanted to keep my record clean. I quickly realized that Sunny was giving me the same interrogation that Mike had given me days before. I didn't deny Sunny an answer. It was proper that he understand who he was allowing into his crew and any addictions that would be a liability to their existence.

While walking the track, Sunny gave me the history on the various characters that we came across. A stocky dark-skinned Samoan inmate came toward Sunny and while still at a distance, Sunny advised me that he was June, a crackhead. I watched as June approached and while he walked at us, he stopped and chatted with at least five different inmates and even exchanged jokes with several officers that walked the yard. June's demeanor matched every addict that I witnessed who had come into the county jail and spent the first week detoxing from drugs. June's clothes were clean and physically he appeared in shape, but the signs that his drug use had overtaken him weren't noticeable in the physical realm— they were in the debt that he had racked up, and the bridges that he had burned in the process.

Sunny didn't have much time for gentle conversation with June as he introduced the two of us. June didn't spend much time on pleasantries as he began his plea for understanding to a less-than-sympathetic Sunny. June constantly shifted his weight, never standing still for more than two seconds—I suppose it was his way to make himself less of a victim if one of his debtors decided that they didn't want to wait for payment. June was desperate to win Sunny over to his side, but it was painfully clear that his pitch wasn't convincing.

June sensed that his company was not welcome, and he found a reason to fade away. Sunny waited for June to walk a good distance away before he filled me in on the severity of June's addiction and how "we would be moving on him soon." I understood the "we" to be the crew that I was a part of. Generally, the Others didn't engage in corporal punishment. But then again, Others generally didn't run debt, as Sunny continued saying as he questioned me, wondering if I used "dope," as he called everything from marijuana to methamphetamine.

Anyone who spent a day confined would understand that there is no individual in prison—there is only your group, and one reckless individual can jeopardize a group's existence. Sunny advised me that June had been given several chances to curb his drug use, and in the past, the group had already paid down his debt, and he had been "red-flagged," which was the equivalent of having a neon light flashing above your head as a warning to all that June was not to be given credit.

We were on the fourth rotation of the track when Sunny advised me that the crew knew who I was—my crime—and they knew about how I performed while in the LA County Jail. There was no subterfuge or fancy ploys to spin a tale. He then advised me that it would be a "good career move" if I stepped up. I understood the severity of what stepping up could entail. I only knew that June had run up debt and had placed the group in danger. June and everyone on the yard knew the consequences of having unpaid debt and June's years of service to the group aside, his current position as a debt-riddled addict meant that he was on the chopping block.

Without committing myself to the task, I had a question for Sunny. I knew that any response would determine my future, or as Sunny put it, my "career," in prison and beyond. So without wasting time, I asked Sunny if I'd have control over how the job would be conducted. Sunny didn't show his pleasure with my question, but I believed I knew Sunny. While we walked the yard, several veteran inmates embraced Sunny with handshakes and congenial words. The respect that was shown between Sunny and everyone that he interacted with made it clear that he had history, and as the days played out, I would be exposed to the sound bites of Sunny's violent exploits. Sunny was sentenced to twenty years with half time in the late eighties, but because of his participation in riots and direct "hits" of enemies, Sunny was just now within a year away from completing the entire twenty years.

I advised him that I was ready to make a move on June when it was time. On the next couple of rotations of the yard, I was introduced to two more guys from our crew. Sam and Marvin had just come from behind the gates where they worked in the main kitchen. Their jobs put them in a position where they could pass messages and other contraband between the yards. To go to their jobs behind the gates meant that they had to submit to full strip searches and examination through metal detectors, so every item they transported had to go to the "hoop" or had to be, as it's commonly referred to, keestered. There was no negotiating that form of transportation for a "kite" because a kite could be a "hot kite" and if it wasn't secured in the hoop then the person transporting it has compromised the message.

This was all information that I was aware of, but Sunny knew that it was his obligation to give me as much information as he could. Sunny had taken me under his wing as one of his older associates had said when he passed us on the track. Sam and Marvin understood that my time with Sunny was necessary and they didn't stay with us long on the track as they allowed Sunny and me to continue our walk.

Once we were alone on our walk, Sunny advised me that Marvin would be rolling with me when I struck at June. Marvin didn't hold much weight and wasn't necessarily a rough-looking guy. He stood at five nine and maybe weighed 150 pounds, but as Sunny reassured me, Marvin had been through a couple of situations where he performed like a beast.

Sunny said that the level of pain inflicted on June would be up to Marvin and me. The only requirement was that he be removed from the yard bleeding. When someone violates his crew's trust and works himself into debt, the crew may choose not to cover his debt and walk away from him, which would throw him to the enemy, or the crew could choose to pay a negotiated portion of his debt and then inflict on him some level of corporal punishment. If a group like the Bulldogs or the Northern Hispanics carried out punishment, their rules stated that the individual would have to leave the yard leaking blood. The extreme rules were meant to serve as a deterrent to other soldiers in their crew.

Sunny introduced two more Others that exited one of the living units that lined the yard. Ben and David were both Puerto Ricans. They both had served time with Sunny, going back to the early nineties when they first met him while in Pelican Bay and later opening High Desert Prison. The trio shared an ease to their interaction that was not present when I watched Sunny interact with Fly, a person that he'd known since their days in free society.

Ben and David were stocky men in their mid-forties. Both had salt-and-pepper sprinkles throughout their facial hair. The differences were in the touches that one could use to state his individual style. Ben wore his hair in a slicked-back ponytail, yet David wore his hair cut close to the scalp where the signs of male-pattern baldness were evident. The pair found ways to individualize their blue prison jeans and shirts; Ben was more tailored and buttoned up, whereas David embraced the hip-hop style, as he wore his clothes in a baggy fashion.

The two embraced me as they cheered knowing that another Hispanic inmate was on the yard that could share in their culture. David immediately asked if I needed anything and before I could answer, Ben chimed in and said that he would put together a care package.

Even though I was embraced by Sunny, the pair didn't know what information I had been exposed to at this point, so in an act of caution David asked Sunny nonchalantly, "How is everything looking with the problem child?" as he referenced the issues that existed with June.

Sunny continued his vigil of the yard as he responded, "He cool. We put together a squad and he gonna get touched up."

The two understood Sunny's words that I was cool to talk business in front of, so Ben asked, "What's the deal with the Dogs?" to which Sunny further put his mind at ease by advising him that Mike had already worked out a payment.

The two were on their way to work in the kitchen on the yard, and the time that they spent getting caught up on the status of June was all that they needed to know, so that they could proceed with their day knowing that our group wouldn't have any issues with the Bulldogs over unpaid debt. The two embraced Sunny and me with handshakes and they carried on, waving to the main tower officer who controlled the gate that would allow anyone to go into the walk area, where they would have access to the administration offices, medical buildings, and their assignment in the yard's kitchen.

Sunny began to tell me how important it would be to know where the tower officer was looking whenever you made a move on someone. His information was for situations even after the business with June was resolved. Sunny pointed out that the main tower has an unobstructed view of the yard and is usually the one who rings the alarm, which causes the officers in the building towers to look out of their windows and respond to the incident. Sunny repeated that whatever business that was being handled on the yard, if there was a weapon involved, if you didn't want to get shot or get a life sentence, then take your shot and get distance between yourself and the weapon.

I surveyed the yard and Sunny began to repeat what Mike had already told me regarding the various ways that the groups divided the yard. Sunny reminded me that the yard had a more militant group of Caucasian inmates that had recently wrestled control from a weaker group of inmates that once regulated the rules for the Woods, so the area that we couldn't walk through covered the basketball courts at the far end of the yard and several tables that surrounded the area. When we made the move on June, we would have to do it between Buildings 4 and 5, where the tower officers in those units couldn't easily eye the action and take a shot with a block gun, or worse, the Mini-14. Luring June into the neutral area would require Sunny or another person in our group to take him for a walk, and when they made their rotation at our area, we would have to strike.

Sunny went on to tell me that he would handle the talk with the Bulldogs and the Brothers on the day that we made our move. Sunny giving the other groups a heads-up was a sign of respect and a way to ensure that they would keep their guys on alert so that they didn't get caught in the chaos that could follow a violent eruption. Sunny made it a point to tell me that he would only tell them on the day of so that June wouldn't get tipped off by a sympathetic Good Samaritan or someone hoping to make him into a rabble-rouser. I didn't have many questions because, sadly, the violent act that I was going to carry out was not a complex task.

Sunny showed me where inmates lined up to go shopping for rations at the cantina and where to look for certain inmates who may be standing for too long in the grassy areas as they could be retrieving or stashing weapons. Sunny took his duty as my guide very seriously. I hadn't had much time to think how I had been on the yard for less than an hour and I had already become part of a conspiracy to inflict serious bodily injury on another inmate. With the rules of prison being instilled by Sunny, and what I knew from movies and my time in LA County Jail, when I made my move on June, I knew that it would be an act that would set the stage for the remainder of my time in prison, and if I were caught, then it could be an act that kept me in prison for the remainder of my life.

The tower officer made the announcement that the yard would be recalled in ten minutes, so without hesitation, Sunny began to move toward the area where Big Ed and Shamu were sitting. I walked in step with Sunny as we came to the table and saw that Shamu and Big Ed were still engaged in their card game but were now joined by two older Brothers. Sunny engaged in small talk with the table as he introduced me to the two Brothers who graciously embraced me with handshakes.

We didn't stay at the table for long as Sunny and I continued our walk toward Unit 4, where I was housed. On the walk, Sunny asked me if I had ever heard of the Soledad Brothers. I told him that I was familiar with the situation of George Jackson and his death as he attempted escape from San Quentin prison. Sunny then told me that the older Brother whose hand I just shook was Ruchell Magee, and while the name didn't sound familiar, Sunny went on to tell me that he was the last surviving member of the group that attempted to negotiate the release of George Jackson during the prison break from the courthouse, as he and several other inmates stood trial for the murder of a correctional officer in Soledad prison. With the assistance of Johnathan Jackson, the younger brother of George, Magee and two other men took five hostages, including the district attorney and the presiding judge, whose head they fixed with a shotgun tied with tape and wire so that it would be like a dead man's trigger if the kidnappers were shot or attacked by rescuers.

Sunny went on to say in a matter-of-fact way that Magee's crew blew the judge's head off when the troops came in to rescue the hostages. The institution and inmates knew that Magee was the figurehead leader of the Black Guerilla Family, but he never, nor any of the other members of the secretive group, dared to admit or allow their membership to be known, or like members of the Aryan Brotherhood, the Mexican Mafia, or the Nuestro Familia, they would be confined to an indeterminate SHU program.

Sunny stopped at the entrance to Unit 4 and advised me that Marvin and I would make the move on June tomorrow during yard. He said that Mike would give me a knife, and when we came out for yard in the morning, Marvin would meet me at the space between Units 3 and 4, out of sight of the tower officers in either unit, and if the guards on the yard were not looking our way when he passed walking with June, Marvin and I could attack him. Sunny said to give the knife to Marvin so that he could dispose of the evidence.

I listened to Sunny and realized that he was giving me the instructions for a potential murder. The intent was to inflict major pain to June, but in the process of driving a piece of metal into his body, I could easily puncture a lung or pierce an artery and if I were caught, I could be setting the stage where my ten-year sentence could become a life sentence.

Sunny asked if I was cool with everything.

I was not in the act of executing hits daily, but after surveying the yard and the straightforward plan that was given, I knew that there was a better chance of escaping the assault if we could contain the action to the blind spot between Units 3 and 4. I knew that there was more to an assault than the assailant forwarding his goal; there existed the real possibility that June could recognize the attack and run or stand and fight.

"Strike fast and get on" was the last piece of advice that Sunny gave before we parted ways.

AVISO!

"If anything in this life is certain, if history has taught
us anything, it is that you can kill anyone."
—M. Corleone

I FOUND MYSELF AWAKE earlier than I would normally rise. I had gone through a stretch routine that had become a part of my morning routine. In between sets, I walked to the window and watched as the night staff walked the tier for their last security count of inmates. The kitchen workers were released from their cells and all appeared to share the same stumbling, half-awake walk. The morning staff arrived and conducted checks of their equipment that fit in slots and holsters at various places on their utility belts. The officers checked the alarms that they would carry throughout their shift.

The morning meal was two boiled eggs with a scoop of oatmeal and a banana. I found myself constantly weighing the superior quality of the meals in prison, which were head and shoulders above what I had to endure for a year in the LA County Jail. I savored the six-ounce carton of orange juice and put to the side the second orange juice that I acquired in a trade for my milk. I surveyed the dining hall and noticed the signs that were posted in English and Spanish that read, *WARNING! NO WARNING SHOTS! AVISO! SIN AVISO!*

I wondered how many of the guys in the dining hall knew that June was up for removal. I wondered if anyone knew that I was a part of the hit team. After catching a couple eyes turn away when I looked in their direction, I reasoned that either everyone knew or I had slipped into a paranoid state. The conscience has an odd way of playing tricks on someone gearing up to commit a crime, and I realized that I was not immune from the anxiety that comes with carrying out an assault under the watch of sharpshooters that have signs posted advising you that when they fire their weapons, the shot is meant to kill you—there is no warning.

Showtime

I WAS BACK IN my cell awaiting the morning program when I noticed China Mike standing at my cell door. I quickly rose to my feet and made it to the door where Mike stood, cool and calm, sipping on his morning tea. Mike had a smile on his face as he asked how my morning was going. I looked at him and he motioned with his eyes for me to look down to a rolled-up piece of toilet paper about the length of my hand. I quickly retrieved the item and Mike waited for my response. I nodded my head and Mike stared me down and offered a simple blessing: "Good luck, brother." And then he walked away.

The tower officer made the call for the unit to be ready for the morning yard movement in five minutes, which meant for me and for June, our lives would forever be changed. I was resolved to my position as the hit man, but I hadn't fully agreed with the consequences that awaited. And just like that, the cell doors opened.

I didn't waste time getting out of the building, but I was sure that I didn't rush so that I became the object that the tower officers focused on. After witnessing many attacks, I had come to see that whatever was out of order, that was what drew eyes. If the yard was full of men walking and I was the only one running, then the tower officer would key in on the anomaly. The normal chatter on the yard of conversations and basketballs being bounced usually came to a pause when something violent took place. Silence was a sign that danger had visited our world.

I stood at the walkway between Units 3 and 4 and was joined by Marvin. We exchanged handshakes and in a low tone, he advised me that Sunny was walking in our direction with June and he wondered if I had the piece. I answered yes and watched as Marvin positioned himself with his back to June and Sunny as they continued in our direction. Marvin told me that when Sunny and June stopped to greet us that he would immediately punch June and I was to follow up his attack by introducing the knife.

Marvin spoke clearly, "Hit him twice in the gut and it's on you how much fun you want to have from there. Then get me the knife and head in the opposite direction…"

I acknowledged that I understood the orders and steadied myself as I noticed that Sunny and June were less than twenty feet away.

The officers were on the opposite end of the yard and the main tower officer was not looking out of his window. The yard's movement had slowed and I imagined that everyone knew that June was on the chopping block. I wondered if June knew, because of his out-of-control drug use, that today was the day that his seventeen years of service to a crew on the mainline were now going to be removed from circulation and potentially cast to a special needs yard.

June and Sunny were now upon us. Marvin began to turn as he heard Sunny say, "What's up, homeboys?" and without hesitation June began to extend his hand in my direction. Having sensed how close June was to him, Marvin unleashed a shot onto June's chin. I immediately moved to June while pulling my knife. Marvin managed to position himself behind June before he could recover from the first punch, and with the grace of a wrestler, he locked down a choke hold, allowing me to extend my knife several times, hitting June in the stomach once and several times in his forearms. June flailed his hands to block himself as I decided to punch him in the face.

June was rendered unconscious and Marvin quickly released him, letting him fall to the ground. Without wasting time, Marvin extended his hand, and I handed him the knife and he stepped in the direction that Sunny walked. I headed in the opposite direction for several feet before turning left where I crossed the grass field. I looked back and noticed that Marvin had caught up to Sunny who had never broken his stride. June remained on the ground with little movement, and the officers had yet to notice that anything had occurred.

While passing Shamu on the grass, he extended an open water bottle and told me to put my hands out as he began to pour water on the blood that covered my right hand, blood that I didn't notice before Shamu pointed it out.

Once the blood was cleared, Shamu and I started to walk farther away from June; then the alarm sounded from the tower and an officer's voice screamed out, "Get down! Get down!" Shamu and I took two more steps before we lay down, never losing focus on where June was on the yard.

Two officers stood over June, who was now lying on his back and holding his stomach. The officers had pulled their batons and kept guard while they waited for the medical staff to respond. More officers ran from buildings and through security gates. Several officers escorted the medical staff who rushed to June, eventually meeting him and quickly placing him onto a gurney.

I lay on my stomach in the tall grass. I examined my hands and clothing and was relieved that they were clear of June's blood, my knuckles free of any bruising. I was nearly in the clear. The only other obstacle was June deciding to give a statement implicating me, or some enterprising inmate who could leverage the information of who the attackers were in exchange for some favor from the administration.

Shamu whispered to me, "You did good, Uce. Shit got to go down sometimes." I nodded my head and observed the medical staff as they fled with June. His entire career as a gangster was reduced to him being carried away as a victim. My prayers were not for June's life, but for myself.

The officers began checking inmates in the immediate area where June had been found. All the inmates were stripped naked and made to bend at the waist while officers ran metal detectors across their bodies. Shamu and I were far enough away from the kill zone so that we were not searched. Marvin and Sunny were in the path that June's gurney traveled, but they too were far enough out of the kill zone that they were not searched either. I wondered if Marvin was able to dispose of the knife. On a yard made up of concrete and metal with sparse pockets of grass, there weren't many places to hide a knife. On Marvin's escape he walked pass the urinals and it was possible that he was able to flush the weapon. The option of tossing the weapon onto the roof existed, but the building's roofs were accessible to officers and a metal knife with a victim's DNA sitting on it would be all the evidence a district attorney would need to proceed with attempted murder charges.

The cluster of inmates in my area was told to rise and walk toward the group of officers that stood in a line searching inmates and releasing them to their respective units. When Shamu and I approached the officers for a search, an officer joked to the other officers, "Here is your hitter right here, the new guy. He got to earn his keep." The group of officers all laughed, but none found it necessary to investigate beyond a cursory search, and once I was examined, I was allowed to return to my unit.

Several inmates were looking out of their windows. Any inmate in the area could've witnessed me attacking June, and the eyes that were on me now could have been people who wanted to get a look at the new guy who made a big move on his second day walking the yard.

Standing alone in my cell and watching the building transform from a sea of officers, who cautiously escorted inmates to a building that resembled a graveyard after the funeral procession has cleared, had sadly become a familiar sight. Once officers "bagged and tagged" the victim and the accused, the survivors—the innocent spectators and the guilty accomplices—were left to deal with the silence of the building as we sat on lockdown, which could last for as little as a day or for months.

I didn't allow myself to feel guilt. A strike against June was necessary and justified, based on the rules of the world I lived in, the world that June had lived in for nearly twenty years. I was a soldier. These were the rules.

All inmates associated with the Others were confined to their cells pending investigation into the assault on June. I viewed Ice as he walked the unit and rambled off high tales about his abilities and his odd retellings of situations that may or may not have happened. Ice found creative ways to keep an audience. I viewed his tales as entertainment and nothing else. *The Ice and Michel Show* is what I named the constant arguments that the two engaged in. The explosive arguments that would have Ice screaming at the top of his lungs, promising Michel that he would kill him, and a day later, the two would be seen scheming over a cup of coffee. This was good theatre, and being on lockdown, this was as good as it got.

Ice delivered a note from Mike.

The note was brief: Good job.

Mad People

"But I don't want to go among mad people," Alice remarked.
"Oh, you can't help that," said the Cat.
"We're all mad here. I'm mad. You're mad."
"How do you know I'm mad?" said Alice.
"You must be," said the Cat, "or you wouldn't have come here."
—Lewis Carroll, *Alice in Wonderland*

WE WERE REMOVED FROM the lockdown on a Saturday, and so I went to the yard dressed in my visiting clothes. I had received a letter from M, who had scheduled time to visit me. The whole time that I was on lockdown, I hoped that the lockdown would be over before this date came. But, like most things in this place, I had little control over decisions that the administration made. Letting go of control was one way to live in confinement without being disappointed.

Mike and I exited the building together and we were greeted by Sunny and Marvin. We exchanged handshakes and hugs as we walked in a group to the table were Shamu and Big Ed were starting a card game. Ed and Shamu stood to greet us with handshakes. Ben, David, and Fly arrived and greeted the group and Fly leaned in and congratulated Marvin and me, without stating what we had done. Sam entered the group and made the rounds with handshakes. Fly decided to ease the mood by advising the group that Suka wouldn't be able to make it to our meeting because he had a "date." The group found that hilarious, as everyone knew that Suka often entertained "clients" in his cell on the weekends. It was not a stretch for Fly to imagine that Suka was in the midst of an affair.

Once everyone exchanged greetings, Fly started the briefing by congratulating Marvin and me on a clean job and giving respect to Shamu and Sunny for their assistance. Fly advised us that June's statements to the authorities didn't implicate anyone. Fly stated that he read the lockup order and June's statement stated that he was hit from behind and didn't know his attacker. Fly went on to say that June's situation was totally his to bear. "He made his bed, and now he is lying in it."

Sam and Mike's names were called over the speaker for visits and the two excused themselves from the meeting, shaking hands as they left. I knew that I had a visit coming and I hoped that there wasn't an incident on the yard, because I was dressed in my visiting clothes and for all incidents, inmates are required to lie out in the prone position—which would ruin my good clothes.

Fly ended the meeting with a reminder for everyone to check themselves and "…no one else will have to…" I realized that Fly was the spokesman for the group, just as Sunny and Mike were. The group structure gave respect to the elders in the group where with the gang-oriented groups like the Northerners, Southerners, Bulldogs, and Woods, the "shot-callers" could be younger than more seasoned inmates—a recipe for possible resentment in a group. Aside from an age disparity, shot-callers may be appointed based on directions from faceless leaders that sit in SHU housing units, who may not fully understand the intricacies of the yard. Which introduced the potential for envy.

The Others and Brothers generally interacted without a set shot-caller. There existed a collegial flow, where the decision-making resembled a democracy instead of a dictatorship, in which one individual and his cronies ruled with an iron fist.

Sunny asked me to "bust some corners" with him, which meant he wanted to walk the track. Part of Sunny's ability to check the status of relationships with allies and adversaries was to walk the track where he would pass the areas where the groups held court. Sunny having me on the walks with him became a tacit approval of my status as a bona-fide convict.

On the walk, Sunny advised me that he was proud of my performance and even joked about how I abandoned the knife and resorted to my fist. He found the effortless transition to be a sign of a "...real gunslinger." I accepted his compliments, but I didn't want to join in a party where I was praising myself for being a gangster, because showing my excitement could set me up to be called upon for any job that arose. I knew that Sunny and the other veterans in the group had been around for decades and in that time, they had sharpened their conversations and interactions with various groups so that they could paint a picture that portrayed pictures as they wanted them to be seen. From the little that I had witnessed with my group, I knew that they were skilled politicians who would have no issue with seeing that their job was completed without having to be the ones who did it.

When walking the track we passed an older, slim-framed Brotha who embraced Sunny with a hug. The older man extended his hand to me and introduced himself as Ruchell. I recognized the man as the person that Sunny had told me about from my first day on the yard; the man who participated in the jailbreak of George Jackson that resulted in the judge being killed as the shotgun taped to his head went off during the escape shootout.

Ruchell appeared strong in mind and his body appeared younger than what I believed he should be in his mid-fifties. His tone was likened to the older inmates that come from the Bay Area—the occasional slurring of words like the accent of someone from the Deep South, and addressing people that he spoke to as "blood," or "young blood." I had imagined that I would interact with someone with more gravitas than the man that I was now walking with. He seemed more concerned with how Sunny's batch of wine was progressing than anything else. At that moment, it became clear to me: these men live here. Although there are moments of great violence and tough negotiations, in the times in between, these men (and myself) live here in a fully functioning society and they are finding ways to make their existence comfortable.

Ruchell and Sunny haggled with a price that would allow both men to walk away from the negotiation feeling as if they had won for the day. In that brief moment I witnessed Sunny's steely focus and what I would later find out, as I walked with Sunny, that by having pleasantries with Ruchell, I was becoming an associate of a man that had the control to order the entire population of Brothas on the inside and the out to strike a target, whether it was an inmate or an officer. I knew that the interaction (and the assumption that Sunny and Ruchell approved of me) could be leveraged moving forward in my prison career—so I planned.

Before we parted ways with Ruchell, who had been summoned to a workout area by associates of his, Ruchell focused his sights on me, and he extended his hand to mine as he lowered his voice, saying, "You did well, young blood. You did well. Congratulations." And with a transition that was effortless, as if he had an internal switch, he turned to Sunny and said, "Are you gonna let me win next time, blood? You've been getting me on these jugs…"

Sunny and Ruchell shared a laugh and a hug as Ruchell walked away playfully pleading with Sunny to give him a better deal in their next deal. Sunny showed his respect for Ruchell as he motioned for me to walk with him as he stood guard while waiting for Ruchell to walk the twenty feet to his associates. Sunny's constant military mindset showed me that he lived in war mode.

Once Ruchell arrived to his associates, Sunny and I turned and began to walk the track. While on the walk, Sunny exchanged greetings with several Hispanic inmates from the Bulldog organization—all extended to me the greeting that was given to Sunny. It was obvious that the violence I committed against June had a positive impact on my profile. It was completely up to me and how I chose to interact with people in business that would determine how I maintained what I had just built.

Once we got out of range of the people that we encountered, Sunny provided me with a profile breakdown. Each person's history was laid bare. I realized that Sunny didn't waste time by entertaining people that he deemed "bitches," or "fuckin' rats" as he never spoke with anyone that he assigned the label of "bitch" or "fucking rat." It was clear that Sunny didn't find it necessary to mince words or be gentle with anyone just for the sake of playing nice. If he didn't like a person, he didn't talk with them. Everyone he spoke to had a positive report at the end of the interaction.

Once we had made a couple of revolutions around the track, Sunny began to tell me about the history of Ruchell and the Black Guerilla Family (BGF). Sunny said that Ruchell realized that he was in over his head when he decided to participate in the escape. He was a teen caught up in the euphoria of the sixties and the idea that George Jackson and his Marxist teachings were the truth and worthy of his blind allegiance.

Sunny went on to list the crimes that the BGF carried out in retaliation for the murder of the cofounder of the BGF and two other African American inmates. Sunny explained how the BGF, on orders from George Jackson, dragged a correctional officer to the third tier of the cellblock and tossed him off with a note attached to his body that read: "One down, two more to go." This murder, and the events that led up to the attempted jailbreak of George Jackson and his comrades, set the stage for what any prison gang would have to do to be feared on the inside and the outside.

In short order, Sunny explained the history of the "BGF's strength…and reach…" when he ran off their crimes; the deaths of correctional officers in Soledad Prison, which were followed by the deaths of correctional officers and inmates during the attempted escape by George Jackson while in Administrative Segregation, where he mysteriously obtained a handgun, before George was killed by a tower officer as he ran into the open area of the yard; the deaths of state correctional officials; and the bombings of police stations and attacks on correctional officers for years to come.

As Sunny explained, the BGF had set the example for any prison gang that wanted to show their influence. But, as other prison gangs worked to meet the BGF's level of violence, correctional officials began to "validate" inmates that they could prove were official members of the main groups—the BGF, the Mexican Mafia (also known as La Eme), the Aryan Brotherhood, and the Nuestra Familia (Norteños). Validation of inmates is an example of a group being too successful in their violence.

Sunny didn't hide his dislike for the Aryan Brotherhood or the Mexican Mafia. Over my time on the yard, while walking with Sunny, he would reveal stories of different wars he'd engaged in against the two groups. In a conversation with Fly, he told me a story of when Sunny was in another prison and the Others and the Brothas were locked in a protracted war with the Southern Mexicans (Mexican Mafia), and Sunny was on a yard that was filled with tense energy, and Sunny, sensing that the Southerners would strike at any moment, decided not to wait around like a victim and retrieved his rusty shiv from his keester. He walked by a group of Southerners and grabbed one of them and stabbed at him several times, leaving the metal shiv in the guy, and turned to the closest guy and knocked him out with one punch before walking away. Apparently the other two guys that were standing in the group chose not to act—a decision that I'm sure cost them their careers.

Sunny made it a point to stress that if I was "ever in doubt, if [I]ever felt that the Southerners were going to make a play, then blast them out of their boots and deal with the rest afterward. It's always better to explain why you made a move than to be looking up at the sky while on a gurney."

With the advice that Sunny imparted to me, I was relieved to know that the way that I believed to be best to get me through this sentence was a way that had provided Sunny the most success for the last twenty years. But he was only set to serve ten years of the twenty years that he was sentenced to. But, he was alive.

My life in prison began to take form. I had a workout routine with Sunny. He and I jogged the track after walking it for enough rotations that it took for Sunny to have conversations with people that bought the wine that he made and other wares that he trafficked in. I returned to the building where I was still housed in a single cell. I laughed at the comedy that Ice and Michel provided as they flirted with violence. I watched the activities on the yard as an observer. Once our business with June was resolved, it was clear that my group didn't have much drama attached to it. The Bulldogs disciplined members of their group secretly and often. The Woods revived their internal war that resulted in two Aryan Brotherhood sympathizers, who were members of the Nazi Lowrider group, to be stabbed by Skinheads and nonaffiliated Woods who were pushing back against the Aryans' power grab. I sat and watched my insanely inventive peers work hard at creating a world that gave them a semblance of the world that we heard about over phone calls, or that were worn on families' faces as they visited, or the world that we viewed through the magical world on our televisions.

From the Desert to the Sea, and all of Southern California...

"This instrument can teach, it can illuminate; yes, and even it
can inspire. But it can do so only to the extent that humans are
determined to use it to those ends. Otherwise it's nothing
but wires and lights in a box."
—Edward R. Murrow

M BROUGHT ME A television and a care package with the basic
items that would serve me on my prison journey—
a chessboard, a deck of cards, tons of chocolate bars, bags of coffee
and tea, pad and paper, hygiene items—for the near future. The
creature comforts were a welcome gift, but I was most excited about
the television, which meant access to the world via the news.

I had devised a schedule that would allow me to view several
morning news programs from around the world before the breakfast
release. The BBC news program from England was a favorite of
mine. Thankfully I was able to view the news on PBS in the early
morning and before the dinner meal. I had several business news
outlets to view from Russian and Asian broadcasts, and the ultra-
liberal media outlets like CBS, ABC, and NBC. I had grown fond of
the local news outlets that covered the San Joaquin Valley and the
folksy way that they covered the news—and the occasional sight of
a shapely street correspondent out in society, covering the local car
theft sting or a press conference with the local police sheriff, who
saw it necessary to provide updates on the most mundane of crimes.

I made my obligatory visit to the yard and performed my workouts with Sunny. The difference in my time on the yard now that I had a television was that I could participate in political conversations that never seemed to end. One ongoing conflict of interest to the older inmates was the conflict in the Middle East and the rising death toll of American servicemen in Iraq.

Up until the arrival of my television, I had limited my participation in current event conversations. I didn't want to chime in on a conversation and be told that I was talking out of my ass and possibly be told that I should shut up. My ego was solidly in place, and I feared how I would react if challenged by someone who didn't care about confrontation, or worse, someone who secretly wanted conflict with me. Sunny and Ruchell held strong views on the latest Israeli-Lebanon war, and if I didn't have the facts to back up my advocacy for either side, then I figured it best to reserve judgment.

Corcoran was in the midst of an oppressive heat wave that had temperatures in the triple digits for over two weeks. Word had traveled throughout the institution that two inmates had died while in the Administrative Segregation housing units. I first heard the rumor from Ice as he walked the tier. It was said that the two inmates died while maintaining an exercise routine. After having seen how rumors take on a life of their own, I knew that it was possible that there was no truth to the tales of the dedicated workout corpses. But I was feeling the oppressive heat and I knew that being confined to a cramped cell without much circulated air would make you feel like you were in a confectionary oven, and you'd wish for the relief of death.

The heat amplified as the sun bounced off the concrete buildings and metal bars covering the yard. The shade from the buildings was a tease and didn't last long, as large portions of it were in the areas of the yard marked out of bounds and in the danger zone.

On the first day that I walked the track with both Sunny and Ruchell, I noticed how many eyes were locked on the three of us.

After my performance against June, the chatter on the yard placed me in the position of a "hitter" for my crew. I was careful not to walk with too much pride. I knew that if I lost a position in a matter, I could be on the receiving end of a bloodthirsty mob, and the same people that I looked past now could be the same people that laughed as I was carted off on a medical gurney.

I was grateful for the hat Sunny had given me the day before, but the hat's brim could only do so much when up against the oppressive sun. As we rounded the track, Ruchell pointed out the group of Bulldogs and Brothers that were playing basketball on this hot day. Just as Ruchell made his assessment of how crazy the group was for going up against the sun, I noticed a gray cloudy figure release from the Brother that jumped for a layup, as his body slammed to the ground. I believed, and Sunny confirmed, that we had just watched this man's soul leave his body.

Several inmates screamed, "Man down!" but no inmate provided assistance once the alarm sounded. Every inmate got a distance from the inmate and complied with the command to lie facedown. There was little rush by the medical staff to aid the man, and even friends of the inmate couldn't be seen providing CPR chest compression to a guy that was lying on the ground for fear that they could be viewed as an attacker. With all the time that had passed, the inmate would surely sustain organ damage of some kind.

The medical officers walked at a glacial pace. Inmates screamed for the nurses to hurry, yet no inmate dared to test the warning signs posted on the walls.

The inmate was carelessly tossed onto a gurney. A male nurse straddled him as he performed CPR while two correctional officers pushed the gurney over the dirt-grass field toward the security gate. The nurse worked hard with one-armed chest compressions while also pushing the balloon end of a face breathing device. Like every other inmate that could've provided assistance, but who was unwilling to test the accuracy of the many tower officers, I felt like a helpless child made to watch as his favorite toy was ripped to pieces by the schoolyard bully. I was denied the ability to move as I wanted, to eat what I desired, and all other creature comforts of a free man, and none made me want to revolt as much as the inability to help another human.

Yet again, like every time before, the officers stormed the yard and searched the inmates in the area where the inmate was found. The yard was cleared and we were quickly sent back to our cells. The rumor mill had begun and within minutes of being in the building I could hear Ice ramble on about the amount of coffee that the inmate consumed on a daily basis and the inmate's use of drugs and the debt that he had left. I didn't know how Ice knew the intimate details of the inmate's collapse, considering that Ice was not on the yard, but Ice had proven to be okay with making up the story as time played on.

I don't have much to add to the death of the basketballer. I didn't even know if he was officially dead. I know that I saw his spirit leave his body as he made his layup shot, and when he lay on the ground there was no sign of life and even though I was at a distance, there appeared to be a peaceful calm to his face.

I focused on the BBC world news and became consumed with the Israeli-Lebanon conflict. The talk on the yard was all condemnation for Israel and what was looked at as a heavy-handed approach to a ragtag militia. Surprisingly, the talking heads on the yard stopped short of tossing anti-Semitic words around and formed opposing views rooted in history and failed US foreign policy.

Having the television would allow me to engage in conversations that up to this point I stayed quiet over when they started. The television was my view into the wider world. Oddly, I began watching *Oprah*, *The Price Is Right*, and every soap opera that came on CBS. *The Bold and the Beautiful* and *The Young and the Restless* were my favorites.

Here I was, a dedicated junkie of information and entertainment. The television allowed me to engage with the outside world. This was all I had, and I accepted it.

Late-night television took the place of a bedtime story. Late, late-night infomercials where scantily clad women with Playboy associations three degrees removed hocked male-enhancement pills and bottles with instant-tan spray guaranteed to take a person from pasty white to mahogany brown. The infomercials also served as material for my late-night solo sessions.

Just when I had become accustomed to life on the Level 4 yard, I received word from Suka that I would be moved to Level 3, B yard soon.

The Kite Runner

"If you want to keep a secret, you must also hide it from yourself."
—George Orwell, *1984*

B EFORE I COULD EXTEND my hand to Sunny who stood outside
of my unit along with Fly, the two of them began to walk, which
was an indicator that time was of the essence and I should follow
their lead. Fly extended his hand and then so did Sunny. Sunny
immediately began to tell me the reason for the immediacy in their
movements as his country drawl sounded off, "You are leaving the
yard soon and comrades have a request…"

I had heard talk from Ice that Suka had a list of inmates that
were set to be transferred and Suka had sent word to me through
Mike that I had to be at yard first thing in the morning, and if I got
called to transfer out of the yard, that I would have to delay until
I spoke with Sunny. I knew that Sunny's desire to speak with me
before I left the yard meant that my services were needed.

Inmates don't move between yards much, so to have someone like
me who is a part of a neutral group like the Others provides a unique
opportunity for someone like Ruchell McGee to deliver instructions
best kept in the deepest of confidences. Having access to another
yard is a major advantage for a group who may want to coordinate an
attack on another group or someone in their group. Whoever carried
the kite would have to carry it internally—in the keester.

Sunny didn't waste time with the talk. Just as I suspected, he
wanted to present to me an "opportunity" whereby I would take

possession of a kite from Ruchell and deliver it to a BGF member on Yard 3. Sunny paused for a second to explain to me how my services were an "opportunity" and not an additional headache and possible way to acquire hemorrhoids. Sunny said the benefit of taking the kite is that it would allow me to know who is a BGF member on the yard I was going to and they in turn would know that I was a "reputable soldier" and an ally that they could call on if there was conflict with the Brothers or with another group.

I understood Sunny's advice and I knew that as much as he insisted it was a decision that was mine, I knew that he hoped I would carry out the task as he stood to gain payment from Ruchell in some form.

I didn't allow too much time to pass from Sunny's advice and my saying that I would carry the kite. Sunny then advised me that once I took the kite, I would be responsible for its delivery. If it were lost— or worse, if I allowed it to be confiscated by the authorities—I would be placing myself in jeopardy. After the warning, Sunny asked me if I was sure that I wanted to proceed as the mule, and without wasting time I answered in the affirmative.

Sunny and I began to walk the track, and as we approached Ruchell, who stood in the workout area of the yard with several of his soldiers, he extended his hand to Sunny and me and then he joined the two of us on a walk around the track. Sunny opened the conversation by advising Ruchell that I was going to carry the kite and added, "If Riley has to destroy the kite to keep it from getting confiscated, then he won't suffer any consequences." Ruchell agreed to the understanding and he extended a half-balled hand to me that contained a tightly bound kite. Without much fanfare I accepted his hand and cupped the kite in mine. Ruchell quickly recommended that I tuck the kite in my mouth for now, but once I get on the move, it would have to be "on the inside."

I knew that I had taken a risk when I agreed to transport the kite for Ruchell. When I got back to my cell, I contemplated opening the kite and reading it. I had heard that the BGF wrote kites in code, so opening the note to read would be an exercise in stupidity, especially if I wasn't able to secure the note in the same creased fashion that it was given to me. Delivering a kite that looked to be tampered with would go against me in the worst way.

I sat on my bunk and thought that maybe what I was delivering wasn't from Ruchell, but was actually a kite from Sunny and Fly to a connection at the yard I was going to and the orders were to strike me, to silence me if I were questioned for the hit on June. I had to consider the possibility. I figured that if they could strike June, a guy they had known for twenty years, then they had the ability to rationalize any act that allowed for them to maintain their dominance, and silencing a loose end wouldn't be out of the realm of possibilities.

My heightened awareness of the many ways a war is waged had me considering all the possibilities I could face. A greeting of hello from a passing stranger or associate could mean anything. I began scrutinizing past interactions with each individual and weighed them against alliances and who I may have had altercations with recently—or long ago. A hello was no longer just a greeting, it had to be examined— the inflection, the tone, and the body language that accompanied them were the only clues to what hello might really mean.

I studied the note and decided that it was a note from Ruchell and it contained information that was the BGF's business and nothing to do with a backstab by Sunny and Fly against me. I gathered a wad of Vaseline onto my left index and middle finger. There was no prescribed manner in which a heterosexual man, who did not engage in anus play as the recipient, would know how much lubrication was necessary so that a note that possibly contained instructions to go to war would easily be inserted. The note was wrapped in plastic when Ruchell gave it to me and I decided adding another layer of plastic was appropriate, considering the compartment that it would be stored in. And with the lightest push that I could get away with, the kite began its journey, as I was on my way to B-Yard, Level 3 of Corcoran Prison.

B-Yard

I ARRIVED ON B-YARD and was assigned to a building that mirrored
the one that I had just left. The yards were all laid out in the way that
allowed for the main tower officer to view all of the living units and
the movements of all the inmates on the yard.

Upon entering, I was greeted by several Samoans who knew my
name. The first inmate that approached me introduced himself as June
Bug from Compton. The name June didn't alarm me as I had come to
know that June was a common name that Samoans embraced. This
June knew of me and my involvement in the attack on his namesake.
Without hesitation, this June embraced me and helped carry my
property to the top tier, where I had been assigned a cell.

The majority of the inmates in the building were assembled
in the unit's day rooms and engaged in the institutional movie
that was playing. The inmates seemed to be in a dream state and
I wondered if I had been assigned to a medical unit where the
inmates were on sedatives.

Several Asian inmates came to the cell where I stood
familiarizing myself with the rules as June and I talked. I exchanged
greetings with everyone that came to greet me. All embraced me
with a handshake and a hug and what seemed to be a genuine
appreciation that there was another soldier for the thin ranks.

I knew that Sunny advised me to deliver the kite to Ruchell's
comrade as soon as I could and that I should ask our people who
spoke for the Brothers, and then I would be able to ask for Johnny from
98 Street in East Oakland, the man that I was to deliver the kite to.

I wanted to relieve myself of the responsibility of holding the kite
as soon as possible. June advised me that the Johnny I was looking for
was in the building and pointed him out with a nod of his head.

I asked June if he would call Johnny over to our conversation
and without hesitation, he moved to get Johnny to my cell door.
I stepped in the cell and pulled the door to a crack and quickly
retrieved the note from myself. I removed the protective layer of

plastic and washed my hands in the sink. The note's original plastic layer never lost its structure and it appeared as creased as it did when I received it from Ruchell.

I noticed June approaching the cell with a tall, muscular man dressed in the same formfitting tank top and baggy gray sweatpants that June wore. Johnny had a pleasant look to his face, and as he approached he extended his hand and stated his name, and I stated mine, and without rushing, I repeated a greeting that Ruchell advised me to say in Swahili: *Habari*, which was my way of asking how he was. Without a second of dead time, Johnny immediately responded as Ruchell advised me that he would with the greeting: *Salama*, meaning peaceful. As Ruchell said, Johnny then would shake my hand and while locked in the handshake, he would tap my middle finger knuckle three times with his thumb, and then repeat the greeting *Salama*.

The exchange happened and without much fanfare. I removed the kite from my back pocket and with the same hand-palm maneuver that Ruchell used when the kite was handed to me, I had relieved myself of it.

Johnny thanked me and asked to be excused. June and I watched as Johnny retreated to his cell where I imagine he sat, decoding orders to eliminate a rival, or the kite was nothing more than a joke, meant to create the illusion that their organization had important business to discuss. Whatever the situation, Johnny didn't waste time in attending to the business of being a member of one of the last of the all-boys club.

June and I entered my cell and he began with the rules of the yard. Unlike A-Yard, where I had just come from, where Bulldog gang members shared the yard with the Brothas and Woods, B-Yard was a mixture of Northerners, Brothas, Southerners, and Woods. The Brothas and Northerners enjoyed an alliance that has endured since the 1960s, when the Woods and Southerners first cliqued to challenge the growing African American prison population and the real-world political gains—inside the prison system and in the wider society—as a result of the civil rights progress.

June gave me a breakdown of the yard's structure and how the real estate was divided. I didn't require much in the way of handholding. June and the other guys in our crew knew who I was and the hit that I participated in while on A-Yard. But as a matter of course I received the basics, and while I unpacked my belongings, June stood vigil and we familiarized ourselves on our individual strengths. I realized June was interviewing me for a position in his administration. Although the Others didn't have a "shot-caller," we did rely on skilled politicians that could avoid war or—in the case of relationships sullied beyond repair—a leader who could lead an army into war.

Once June left, I knew that if I was going to have any say in how my life would be lived in the years that I had ahead of me, then I would have to take on a leadership position and have a say in the group. Stepping up to lead would allow me to exercise some form of control in my life where since my arrest, I'd had little. Since my incarceration I had morphed into an observer, nothing more than a pedestrian waiting for the traffic cops to point at where I should travel. Other groups of inmates had imposed their gang associations on the population while I was in the Los Angeles County Jail and my group was forced to associate with the Brothers as a way to survive. But, upon entering the Department of Corrections, I saw the independent status of the Others and I was relieved that my decisions up to this point had placed me in a position where I could have a say as to what I would do, and to whom.

I didn't want to make a career out of this life. One of the jokes that flowed from June when we were familiarizing ourselves with one another was his comment about an older Cambodian inmate that had returned to the unit from work. The inmate was incarcerated on his eighth parole violation and June properly described the guy as being on the "lifer-installment plan" with CDC, yet he was the only one who hadn't figured it out yet. I didn't want to be that guy. I just wanted to survive this journey and return to my world.

I sat in my cell that night and wrote to my mother for the first time in a while. I wrote few people as I didn't have many updates that I wanted to share with anyone in the outside world. I didn't have much I could say, beyond an apology. My decisions had caused suffering in many lives, and all I could do at this stage was lighten the burden of concern by allowing people to know the few pleasures of this world that I had some control over—my mental and physical health—and to deny them any idea of the suffocating feeling that consumed me.

After signing off on the letter to my mother, I scribbled the most basic of letters to L. I had continued to write to her at the last known address I had for her. She had never written back, and the letters were never returned undeliverable. My letters to her were once in the thousand-word range, but now I could barely devise a note that could fill up a page. Beyond the standard proclamations of love, I no longer had much to share. The one-way love affair that I had been engaged in had reached its end.

I signed the letter, "Love, Riley" and started on my next letter to M. I thanked her for deciding to take the walk with me through hell. I didn't know how far she would make it, so with forethought for the struggles ahead, I asked if she would have patience with me as I knew that I was not fully in control of myself. I knew that I was fortunate to have a friend in M, but I also knew that having someone to care for also served as a burden. If I only had to consider myself, making decisions that could place me in lockup or worse would be simpler. Only I would bear the weight of any consequences. Having family and friends to consider would make these decisions much more difficult.

Yard

I WALKED OUT INTO the concrete yard with the oppressive heat that blanketed the prison and the outside world, yet I couldn't shake the thought that this prison yard had received more of the burden. The officers in the tower bared the same Mini-14 rifles that I had become accustomed to walking under. The same inmates that populated the

Los Angeles County Jail, the reception center, and A-Yard all existed at my new residence. It was a relief to see that inmates didn't become possessed with superhuman strength upon entering prison as the tall tales of scared inmates in the county jail would have you believe. Man, it was hot.

I saw individuals that reminded me of the head of the construction crew that I worked in the summers. I saw the man that looked like the guy that changed my tires a week before my arrest. The older grey-haired judge type of guy was represented in this world in equal numbers as the juvenile delinquents that filled the inner city. The inmates were merely men. Men that had violated laws that other men wrote. Laws that they agreed to abide by. We were all dressed in blue and carried a number attached to our names.

Here I stood with men that were prepared to kill to save their lives from imaginary enemies. I knew that if I was going to survive that I would have to match their resolve at a moment's notice. The men that had become my enemies by virtue of their ethnicity or gang affiliation had realized that their existence was far more important than mine, and they had adapted to the realities of the world that we lived in. This was life—not a perfect one, but the life that I was living—the life that I had made for myself.

I had asked myself the question "What is real?" several times since I started this journey. I was now at a different stage of life to find the answer. It was clear to me that where I was in life was just another stage and not the end, but I had come to know what was real.

This yard would be my world, and the dingy brick walls and barbwire fences with armed officers walking the catwalk served as a reminder that any romantic notion of an early release by way of escape was not an option. Man, it was hot.

THE END.

ACKNOWLEDGMENTS

TWO YEARS INTO MY ten year sentence I decided to roll the numbers that were salvaged from my former life and placed a call to an old friend, Scott Caan. I didn't know how he would receive me, considering the many crimes that had been attributed to me. There was a part of me that didn't want to cast a shadow on anyone in the free world, and a collect call with a mechanical operator made it known that I was incarcerated. A chill could take over for anyone that may have been warm to accepting communication. But, in short order, Scott answered; pushed the correct buttons to accept the call, and immediately delivered me the sharpest rebuke of my failed attempt to rule by force: "You crazy motherfucker, what the fuck did you think was going to happen; you snatched the dude in Bel Air." For the next fifteen minutes I answered the obligatory questions that any civilian would have when speaking with a convict: "Are you working out; have you stabbed anyone; do you have a girl in there, or are you some one's bitch?"

I had known better than to be solicitous with the details of my confinement, due in part to my experience with L as she tried to salvage a relationship with me and the pain that Frankie endured as he outlasted L's time in my life. I had resolved to be a pleasure to be heard from. My stories to anyone that chose to be in my life would be about "after" this experience ended and not my present dilemma.

No matter how I presented my resolve for a life past confinement, the call with Scott was interrupted every five minutes by the mechanical operator reminding him that I was incarcerated at Corcoran State Prison. The last reminder being a notice of one minute remaining on the call. Scott asked me, "What are you writing?" and my response was, "I had nothing." I didn't want to lay the burden on his mind with the truth that it would be hard for me to keep a journal where I discuss the latest assassinations on the yard.

Scott reminded me, "Write. Write, whatever comes up. It's your experience." That became a line that he bestowed on me when I called over the next seven years. "Keep writing," and that is what I did. Once released, I unified my notes into the words you're reading and then handed it off to Scott with a reminder that he encouraged me down this path.

Scott handed the manuscript to Tyson Cornell at Rare Bird who had recently published Scott's book, *The Performance of Heartbreak and Other Plays*. Scott warned me that the publishing world works on its own clock and "if Tyson says he wants it, then that's his word, it'll get done."

I'm eternally grateful to you, Scott, for reminding me that I was living a situation that others needed to know existed. Tyson, I thank you for taking a chance on this Neanderthal man.

After reviewing the list of authors at Rare Bird, I knew that my thoughts would be comfortably accepted. You placed me with Guy Intoci, an editor that would've been a persuasive leader in any profession, but, thankfully he chose literature over flirting with the notion that he could've pulled off any of the crimes that I've been accused of (even though you are persuasive, it would've been a tough ride for you on the yard).

Julia Callahan, from day one we bumped knuckles over our respective love for the Giants and Dodgers and it was clear to me why Tyson has you to keep the bird on course.

To my brothers, Alex Vaysfeld and Frankie Liles, I am grateful for your steadfast support. Jerry Rosenburg and Doc Holliday, your support and laughs sustained me through the years. Tony

Riviera, the only time you said no is when I returned to LA and you wouldn't allow me to wash dishes in your restaurant. I told you any illusion that I may have had where washing dishes was a job beneath me left me the first time that I was ordered to bend at the waist for an inspection of my sphincter. Your reasoning was simple: "write." Anthony Riviera, you've been a friend. Will Wright, even with your miscalculations, you stepped up when your back was against the wall. Ron Richards, James Epstein, and Frank DiSabatino, you all are the embodiment of competent counsel that the Sixth Amendment guarantees.

Pat Robinson, Joe Calhoun, Kolani Togafau-Fiti, Tee Luafale-mana, and many more that walked the same yards with me, I have many thanks for you friendship.

To my love, Jennifer Morgen, I am honored to have met you and for you showing me what is real in love. You've faced opposition to our relationship and you always returned to the man that you know and not the one whose transgressions were litigated in decades past. When it has looked like we were alone, you returned to love. Thank you Ivy Frances Morgen for accepting me without conditions. It was never by the book, but that is life.

Peter Conti, Andy Fiscella, and Rob Weiss, I appreciate your friendship and your counsel. Michael Corrente, James Acheson, Slaine, Jake Rohn, Nate Blonde, Jeff Santo, Lorenzo Antonucci, Dina and Fred Leeds, Susanna Macias, Ray and Walter Rodriguez, Liam Hayes, Jackie and Skip Morgen, Raina, Brighton, Breelayne, Blake and James Ring, Dwight "Heavy D" Meyers (RIP), Casius Green, Jeremy Valdez, Mike "Bounty" Hunter (RIP), Charmelle Smiley, Betty Banks, Herman and Maria Hibler, Chanerrick Tisdale, Lamont Nixon, Zevi Kreiner, Vivian McCord, Terri and Jaime Weinberg, I am thankful for your love and acceptance. Rabbi Chaim Mentz and Rabbi Levi Cunin your wisdom is greatly appreciated. To L and M, in our interactions, I've learned a lot. Thanks for the experience.

To my mother, Azline Kathryn, who has walked with me through hell, whatever remains will be better. I love you. My brother Ray, I look forward to the day that we are reunited with Earl. A very special thanks to my dear friend Leon "BO" Simpson, I wish you could've read this.